Peeling Point —

Usually when — keep
running through it
until you don't
die

You can any body/PR
they talk about "taking their social destiny into
their own hands" + reorganize the bottom line

It is extremely general + yet is meant
focussed on a particular readership.
Business — 3 piece suit type
Businessmen might type
who need to be given
the book + possibly
convinced or to
ready it.

... surrender to the joy of
    profreading ...

my story —

Donna's too the dream / the
held on it while used   either

the second of
here can be
is chosen
Let go / needs + it's
It's
14 be L when in doubt
        let go
chap 15

Creative
vacuum

... others

167

2/3

2/5

WINNING BY LETTING GO

Elizabeth Brenner

HARCOURT BRACE JOVANOVICH, PUBLISHERS

San Diego   New York   London

Winning by Letting Go

CONTROL WITHOUT COMPULSION, SURRENDER WITHOUT DEFEAT

HBJ

Library of Congress Cataloging in Publication Data
Brenner, Elizabeth, 1954–
Winning by letting go.
1. Control (Psychology)   2. Social control.
3. Self-control.   4. Subconsciousness.   I. Title.
BF632.5.B74 1985   153.8   84-25152
ISBN 0-15-197130-7

Designed by Amy Hill
Printed in the United States of America
First edition
A B C D E

*To my mother, Grace Brenner Collins, who
gave me the best of both nature and nurture*

Eternal vigilance is the price of freedom.
                    —Thomas Jefferson

Contents

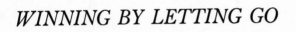

WINNING BY LETTING GO

1 ALWAYS THE QUESTION: TO HOLD ON OR LET GO?

"I want to go back to school, and you can't stop me," stormed Janet to her husband. "Every time I try to do something for myself, you say I'll get hurt or it won't work. Quit trying to tell me what to do!" Her husband, Sam, did not see himself as trying to control his wife. In fact, he considered himself a liberated guy. It was just that every time she was out of his reach, he felt uncomfortable and started to "worry" about her. His seemingly good intentions were based on an anxious need to control her. Janet tried to explain this to him many times, but he could not understand what she wanted from him. Finally, after eighteen years of marriage, she left him to return to school and start her own life. His inability to let go of his wife a little by supporting her in her education and growth ultimately led him to lose her completely. What appeared to be a conflict over lifestyle and education had much more to do with control. How might this story have ended if Sam had been able to let go more in the first place?

From his office at Twenty-second and K streets in Washington, D.C., Kay McMurray directs the Federal Mediation and Conciliation Service, the mediator of last resort for labor negotiations in the United States. He helped settle the 1983 Greyhound strike and has played a crucial role in the resolution of many other major labor disputes. In discussing control and surrender with me, he said, "How do I deal with a person who has an overdeveloped need to control? It's easy. First I take him aside and tell him what he's doing and what a damaging effect he's having on the negotiations. I ask him to cut it out. Then we go back into the negotiations, and if he keeps on pressing for control, I call the chairman of the board of his organization. The chairman has a talk with him, and after that he usually changes his attitude; if not, he is often removed." Overdeveloped control needs are counterproductive, both in organizations and in personal relationships. Those who are truly in control don't push for it: Their control speaks for itself.

Jerome, a young negotiator working for a major film studio, strode into his meeting with Steve, an agent who represents a powerful independent film producer. He represented the powerful studio, so he assumed that he could set the terms of the negotiation. Overconfident of his position, he had neglected to do his homework: The producer could probably work wherever he wanted. "Here's what we'll give you for him, Steve," he said to his counterpart at the agency, "take it or leave it." Steve, who knew what his client wanted and what he could get if he bargained for it elsewhere, replied easily, "Fine, we'll leave it." Stunned, Jerome left his office thinking that perhaps Steve was bluffing. When he later found out that the producer had gone to another studio and gotten exactly what he'd wanted, he was furious. He had overestimated his own control, made a foolish ultimatum, and lost.

George Ball served as a close advisor of American presidents from Roosevelt to Carter. During the Vietnam War, he was the first—and for a long while the only—top-ranking diplomat who maintained that the United States would be better served by executing a tactical withdrawal than by pressing for victory. History has proven him correct. I talked with him at his home in Princeton, New Jersey, where we discussed the conflict between control and surrender that went on in the White House during the Vietnam War. "During the whole war, there was a common theme repeated first by Johnson and then by Nixon in exactly the same language: 'I will not be the first President to lose a war.' On one occasion I pointed out to Johnson that that wasn't true, that we hadn't won every war, and that made him very cross. He liked to think that this was a country that always won anything it got into and that he was going to uphold this tradition. I kept telling Johnson that no great captain in history has ever been blamed for a well-calculated tactical withdrawal. One must get out of an untenable situation rather than stumble on aimlessly. In fact, I wrote him a long paper once in which I proposed that we try to develop a doctrine of extrication, that we had doctrines for doing everything else in wars except getting out of them."

The tragedies of Vietnam, both personal and national, could have been reduced if the leaders and the people of the United States had known when to let go.

Think of all the ways that you have used, or seen used, to exert control. Screaming, pummeling, throwing vases, threatening to beat or injure someone, manipulating, wheedling, demanding, complaining to someone's boss, crying, withholding food or affection, refusing to meet someone's terms until he meets yours, pretending not to hear what someone is saying—the list goes on and on. Notice the reactions you get from people when you use these means of control: They comply through fear, they are angry. These are the kinds of control that ultimately don't work.

People in every part of society use these techniques to try to gain control over others and over situations they care about. Parents use them against children, children use them against parents, husbands and wives use them against each other. Soldiers, policemen, politicians, business people, merchants, schoolteachers, and religious leaders: All have, at some time, tried to drive a fishhook of control into those around them, regardless of the damage they are causing. Even the pleasantest among us has used this aggressive and dominating approach to control. We do this because we think it is the only way we can get what we want.

Attempting to dominate and exert authority may give us a momentary feeling of control. But is this true control? Is control through domination the best we can hope for? Or is it possible that we might win by letting go?

In writing this book, I interviewed some of the most powerful business people in the country. To my surprise, each one of them said that the best way to gain control is, in some way, to let it go. You could fill a library with books about controlling through force and manipulation. We don't need another one. This book is about control through surrender, control by knowing when and how to hold on, and when and how to let go. And it is about pure surrender —not the miserable defeat so feared by many, but a dynamic and joyful choice to go *into* life.

Conflicts between controlling and letting go spring up everywhere in our lives. The way we respond to them has a clear impact—both in costs and rewards—on our business and personal lives. Mark, a surgical resident in a large university hospital, groaned as the nurse shook him awake from a brief nap. "An emergency has just arrived." Fumbling with his clothes, he tried to clear the accumulated fatigue of months of interrupted sleep from his mind. Someone's life depended on his alertness. After washing his face and downing a cup of coffee, he felt ready. The patient, a fourteen-year-old boy, had been thrown from the back of a friend's motorcycle during a late-night joy-ride. Mark and his team worked on the boy all night, urgently clamping and stitching. Finally, at 5:00 A.M., they felt satisfied that he would make it. Mark returned to his room for an hour of sleep before rounds. When he awoke, the head nurse informed him that the boy had died.

"I felt awful," he says, "I felt I was ultimately responsible for his death. I know I shouldn't, but I kept thinking there was something else I should have or could have done." He felt that part of his job as a conscientious doctor was to use his surgical skill to master injury and disease. It was a tremendous challenge for him to use his control wisely and then let go when he had to. He was forced to accept the limits of his control and be fully, compassionately present for each patient without attachment to the patient he'd just left.

Those of us who attempt to ward off the uncontrollable Fates are bound to be frustrated. Sooner or later and despite our best efforts, something happens that is beyond our control, and we feel anger, frustration, and loss. If we are able to accept those feelings and then release ourselves from the emotions and expectations we're grappling with, we are free to move on—growing from our experience without letting it hold us back.

WHO'S IN CHARGE?

> If you will be observant and vigilant, you will
> see at every moment the response to your action.
> Be observant if you would have a pure heart,
> for something is born to you in consequence of
> every action.
>
> —Mevlana Jelalu'ddin Rumi,
> thirteenth-century Sufi
> mystic[1]

When we use the word "I," we are saying that we recognize someone as being "ourself," someone different from the person next to us. Although we may not realize it when we use the word casually, as in "I did the job" or "I think it's too hot to work today," we are identifying ourselves by particular criteria. Among the most basic of these "me-identifying factors" are our name and our body. In reply to the question, "Who are you?", I might say, "I'm Elizabeth Brenner. I'm tall and have auburn hair." This only tells the other person my name and certain details about my physical appearance, but somehow it seems to answer the question. We also define ourselves by our family relationships, the way we dress, the way we think, the way we feel, our opinions, the memories of everything that's happened to us, and so forth. Without realizing it, we experience this combination of body, name, thoughts, feelings, and memories and call it "me." This way of identifying ourselves is perfectly adequate for most day-to-day speech and thought.

If we believe or act as though this collection of factors is all there is to us, however, we are missing something. There is also an "observer" in us that views everything going on in our body, heart, and mind. It's the part that's always watching us do what we do. You know that part of yourself. It's watching you read this book right now. The observer in us sees everything with equanimity; it sees all our circumstances from a broad perspective. The observer is distinct from the "object self"—the collection of "me-identifying factors" that we just spoke of.

While this may seem like an abstract philosophical distinction, it can be enormously helpful in solving problems in our daily lives. If my business is on the verge of bankruptcy and my marriage is on the brink of dissolution, or if I am simply lonely or upset, it is important that I *know* that I am more than my thoughts, feelings, and circumstances. Rather than suffer through an endless succession of mental and emotional upsets, I can see my life from the viewpoint of an objective observer rather than a frenzied participant. Clear observation enables me to see things as they are, to notice which factors *can* be changed, and which *must* be changed, to get me through this crisis. Then I can act firmly and appropriately. Not only in times of intense crisis but also when dealing with any question or conflict in life, switching to the observer's point of view takes me out of the whirl of circumstances and into balance. The Greek mathematician Archimedes said that if only he had a place to stand, he could move the world. The observer in us, within ourselves yet outside the subjective world of thoughts, feelings, and beliefs, is our "place to stand."

The object self–observer distinction is helpful in discussing control and surrender. If we believe that the object self is all there is to this person we call "me," then the prospect of surrender may seem frightening. However, when we realize that we are more than we may have given ourselves credit for, that someone would remain if we did "surrender" or let go of a particular thought, feeling, or situation, then the prospect of letting go seems less fearsome. In our discussion of the way he works, Jay Olins, president of California Student Loan Finance Corporation, said, "By not getting caught up in a crisis, you function more efficiently. The best way . . . is to move yourself out of the situation and look in at it from the outside." This ability to "step outside" of situations and deal with them dispassionately has helped him build his organization into a multimillion-dollar enterprise.

No matter how embroiled in our ego we become, the observer is always instantly available; as dispassionate and "observant" as we are at any time, we can slip into object-self perspective instantaneously. We may be gliding through a traffic jam with Buddha-like equanimity and then suddenly feel like honking maniacally at the slow driver in front of us. There is no time or distance lapse between the observer and the object self. Both are always present, and we're always functioning from the perspective of one or the other. Neither is superior. What I suggest we aim toward is smoothness of transition between object and observer—and between control and surrender. This lets us choose, moment by moment, what is necessary to complete the task at hand.

Here are some of the differences in the ways that control and surrender appear to the object self and the observer within us:

Object Self	*Observer*
Control as effort, resistance, negation, barter	Control as effortless, appropriate modulation of activity
Surrender as loss, capitulation under duress, defeat	Surrender as glad acceptance, letting go, release

Our feelings about control and surrender vary, therefore, depending on the point of view we adopt.

ARE WE REALLY IN CONTROL
TO BEGIN WITH?

Many of us *feel* that we are out of control or at least that
we have no real control over what happens in our daily
lives. Actually, we have tremendous control over what
happens to us moment by moment, but if we believe in our
lack of control fervently enough, all our experience will
justify that belief. When we are willing to acknowledge
and take charge of our natural ability to control, we feel
an instant increase in our sense of power and self-worth.
Millions of dollars are generated annually by "motiva-
tional" speakers who simply encourage their listeners to
believe that they can meet those sales goals, buy those
condos, or do whatever else they had thought was beyond
them. When we change our beliefs and expectations, we
change our experience, so believing in our ability to control our lives increases the amount of control we feel.

If forces are uncontrollable, we'll find out about them
whether we like it or not; we really don't have to worry
about them. What's more important is accepting the reality
of the uncontrollable and then forging ahead with what we
can control. But most of us have dispossessed ourselves of
much of our capacity for control—we have buried it. What
covers it? Often, an unwillingness to confront the paradox
that we are both completely in and completely out of
control.

In surrender, a similar paradox confronts us. We may
fear surrender, believing that letting go or giving in will
be the end of us. Then when circumstances force us to let
go, we often experience relief that surpasses any joy that
controlling ever gave. We forget that surrender is at its
root a *voluntary* act, something we choose to do.

Each of us has dealt with questions of control in his
own way; each of us has also found his own ways of letting

go. Some of these ways have worked; others have not. No matter how or why we'd like to change the way we deal with control and surrender, we have to begin by seeing and accepting how we deal with them now. Are there any times when you might have been more satisfied if you had dealt with holding on and letting go in a different way? Rather than asking "What do I need to change?" ask yourself, "How can I let myself grow?" You may find new ways to answer this question in the pages to come.

In exploring control and surrender, we will come face to face with paradox and previously unexamined beliefs and fears. By doing so, we will discover that our capabilities are vastly beyond what we might have thought. Control and surrender already permeate our lives. What we'll do together in this book is look into them a little more thoroughly for our own benefit and the benefit of those we love.

2 WHAT IS CONTROL? WHAT IS SURRENDER?

In July 1983, the investment world was stunned by the unexpected announcement that Peter G. Peterson, chairman of the board and co–chief executive officer of the prestigious firm of Lehman Brothers Kuhn Loeb, was voluntarily relinquishing both his positions, to be replaced by his co–chief executive officer, Lewis Glucksman. Peterson had joined the firm in 1973 and within weeks had been asked to take over as chairman. At that time the firm suffered from internal division, substantial losses, and a relatively fragile financial base. During the ten years he was at the helm, Peterson rebuilt Lehman Brothers into a powerful, respected, highly profitable, and widely diversified investment institution. When he announced his resignation, speculation was rampant in the business community that Peterson had in fact been forced out; few people could believe that a man holding such an influential position could voluntarily give it up. But accounts from those closest to the story indicate otherwise.

Peterson had volunteered in May 1983 to share the chief executive officer's functions with Glucksman; there was no sign of any discontent on Glucksman's part at that time. Soon afterward, however, he came to Peterson and said that he had realized that he would not be happy unless he had complete control of the firm. Diplomat George Ball, a partner at Lehman Brothers, was called in as a friendly mediator in the negotiations between Peterson and Glucksman. In my discussion with Ball about the change in leadership, he said, "There was a large element of statesmanship in Peterson's decision. He didn't consider the problem solely in terms of the short-term consequences or solely in terms of his own welfare and advantage. He took into account the interests of a major institution. Peterson had had the control for ten years, and he had built the firm. He had been contemplating the possibility of a move within a few years, perhaps a gradual relinquishment of his responsibilities, so what he was in effect doing was speeding up his own timetable."

In a telephone interview from his Manhattan apartment, Peterson himself said, "This is hard for some people to grasp, but there are some situations in life where winning is losing. My wife and I tried to think through what was really meant by winning. If by winning we meant getting a lot of partner votes but somehow leaving the institution hurt, or having to repeat another long-term rebuilding commitment I wasn't prepared to make, well, I didn't call that winning.

"You know, a business colleague of mine, a Greek in American business, said that if anyone ever confronted him with a sudden desire to assume full responsibility on an accelerated time schedule, he would have immediately gotten involved in a conflict. It would have to be a conflict just because there was a demand and a challenge to his authority. He said to me, 'I guess that's the difference between a man from Sparta'—meaning him—'and a man from Athens'—meaning me."

Subsequent events proved the value of "Athenian" versus "Spartan" control. Within three months of taking over Lehman Brothers, Glucksman himself was forced out in the course of the company's takeover by American Express. As *Newsweek* reported in its issue of April 24, 1983, "After Glucksman took over, . . . he set out to assert a measure of control over the various Lehman fiefdoms. . . . One Lehman official says that to Glucksman, control meant 'independent partners being brought to their knees.' " Glucksman offended established members of the company by putting men from his special area, trading, into high-echelon posts and by taking a disproportionate share of company profits for himself and his cohorts. *Newsweek* went on to say that "he took responsibilities away from some Lehman stalwarts and arbitrarily moved others to different departments to dilute their bases of support. Not surprisingly, many people quit the firm. . . . The directors ran out of patience last January, when Glucksman forced the election of Robert Rubin, another trader, as the firm's president. Glucksman was told by several directors at a long and contentious meeting that the job should go to an investment banker experienced in dealing with clients outside the firm—in other words, someone who could fill Peterson's old role. Glucksman won the day but lost his future. The other directors were so incensed at his stubbornness that they regrouped—and decided the man had to go." How often have individuals who sought raw control without considering the consequences won the day but lost the future?

One often sees people at the highest levels of business and politics wanting control and having it; to know when to give it up and how to let go gracefully may be a sign of greatness. As Malcolm Forbes, publisher of the respected financial magazine *Forbes* and the 1983 Publisher of the Year, told me, "You keep control only by having confidence in those you give responsibility to and letting them exercise it. By giving away control, you keep it."

We all have ideas about what control is. This is not

surprising; we certainly hear enough about it. Weight control, pest control, control of blood pressure, price control, control of the Senate and the House—control is a popular thing to have. Look at the incredible popularity of figures like the fictional Godfather, who seemed able to counteract the forces of fate and give people "green cards" from the Department of Immigration, jobs, even life. The Godfather had control, the President has control, the boss has control. In some ways, each of us feels he has some control.

Many of us think we know what surrender is, too. There's Old West surrender, with long-faced cavalrymen throwing their guns at the feet of the Apaches as a white flag rises over the fort; or Japanese surrender, with the Emperor declaring at the end of World War II, "The war has developed in a way not entirely to our advantage" (a classic example of understated surrender). An advertising campaign for a candy bar was once built around the slogan "Don't Fight It—Surrender." Then there are the sensuous surrenders hinted at in advertisements for cognac and cologne—a young woman in a revealing black evening dress flings herself into the arms of a handsome (but still controlled) man and whispers, "Take me, take all of me! I'm yours." Slow fade-out. On top of these worldly surrenders are the mystical surrenders of great poets and saints, who write ecstatically of abandoning themselves utterly to God or religious service. Surrender can be a humiliating defeat or a blissful deliverance. How can it be so many different things to so many different people?

"Surrender" originates in the idea of fully rendering or giving over to someone else. The French term for surrender is a reflexive verb, *se rendre*, that literally means "giving oneself over." This begins to give us a sense of how surrender can be at once so desirable and so abhorrent. It all depends on what we choose to give ourselves over to. Depending on its object, surrender can be a dynamic expansion, voluntarily letting go of the old in favor of the new.

Control is also a matter of choice—of freely deciding to use our personal power for doing what works best. The executive who sees to it that his employees complete their work on time is using control; so is the mother who refuses to give a child dangerous tools before he's old enough to use them safely. Anyone who turns away from an insult rather than start a fight is exerting control. Control can be a positive application of energy and will, creating and making things happen, or it can be negative, applying the same energy and will to prevent something from happening.

The traditional view is that the best way to "win" in life is by retaining maximum control over ourselves and others. However, there is a difference between control through domination and manipulation, and control through surrender. As we will see, control through surrender means allowing processes to play themselves out, all the while guiding them in the direction we'd like them to take.

You have already experienced surrender, although you might not have called it that. What we are examining here is how to extend this capacity and why we might want to develop our surrenders from small to large; from surrender with an object to transcendent, objectless surrender; from surrender as passive acceptance to active surrender to life. Each step, each level, is valuable, and each has its own risks and rewards.

FACE IT: YOU CAN'T
CONTROL IT ALL

Many people associate control with winning and surrender with defeat. Some might say that control by domination is sufficient and that if we can lord it over ourselves and others, we'll have all the control we want or need. But this overlooks a crucial fact: There are *real* limits to our control.

Gravity controls our ability to fly. Death controls our capacity for immortality. Except in certain small parts of the globe, the changing seasons control our ability to plant and harvest crops whenever we please. The person who sees and accepts the controls imposed by reality has already increased his own control, even if the reality is that he has little control.

In any negotiation, each party has some control, but one has more "real" control than the other. You may have a big advertising budget to assign, and I may represent one of fifty agencies competing for it. In this case, you have control in the form of power and money. However, I have something you need—talent and ideas. If I barge into our meeting as though I were the boss, I will probably lose. However, by accepting the situation and providing what you—the boss—want, I may win the bid and emerge from the negotiation having the more important kind of control, *control over results.* One party may have more control at the outset, but it's more important to see who has control at the end. Young David had little control in the form of physical power when he first faced Goliath, but he got control when it counted. Thus, control is power, not only the static power of commercial or material resources but also the active power to make things happen.

So far, we've looked at three different aspects of control: control as domination, control as material or political power, and control as having things turn out as we want. It's because most of us are so fond of this third aspect that control is so popular.

However, most of us realize early on that things do not always go our way. True control, as we'll be viewing it in this book, does not mean having the power to invariably have our way. It begins with the capacity to *see* things exactly as they are, and develops into the capacity to *choose* how to *deal with* things as they are.

Sally, a pediatric nurse and single parent, was told that her fifteen-year-old daughter, Colleen, had cancer of the lymph glands. She knew that chances of survival were good but that the girl's life depended on undergoing painful radiation therapy which might make her incapable of bearing children. Of course if Sally were in full control of the universe, she would have ordered that her child not get cancer in the first place. But she wasn't. Together, mother and daughter had to choose whether to resist the realities of the disease and avoid treatment or to accept them and control the course of the disease as best they could. Their "cancer control" consisted of

1—*Accepting facts*
2—*Knowing what they could (and could not) control*
3—*Focusing on a priority goal (in this case, keeping Colleen alive)*
4—*Doing what was necessary to reach the goal (having the radiation therapy)*

Colleen accepted the therapy, and although she paid a high price in terms of her fertility, she accepted it as the price of survival. As Jewish community leader Susan Lapin says, "We can accept that a serious illness is the will of God and not fight against the fact but still fight against the disease. Part of overcoming it is accepting it."

Refusing to accept the limits of reality robs us of all further control. A woman in her early forties, Joanne is a metaphysically oriented psychotherapist. She is afraid of doctors and believes that most Western medicine is a sham. When she started seeing haloes around people, streetlights, headlights, and lamps, she was excited at the thought that her "psychic vision" was finally opening up. "I can see

auras!" she told her husband. "Maybe, but it could also be
a problem with your eyes," he suggested. "Why don't you
go to a doctor just to be sure?" "I don't want to go to the
doctor—my vision is fine," she insisted. Six months later,
she awoke one day to find that she was blind in one eye.
Advanced glaucoma had already caused irreparable nerve
damage to that eye; she is currently struggling, with the
help of *lots* of doctors, to retain her failing vision in the
other. There was a physical basis to her problem. She ignored reality and by doing so squandered the time that
might have been spent in treatment to save her sight. People who ignore the controls of reality can temporarily pre-
serve their illusions, but in the end they slam unprepared
into an impassive wall of facts.

THE BASIS OF CONTROL
AND SURRENDER

While control and surrender may at first appear to be op-
posites, they have a common basis: the clear recognition
and acceptance of facts. In terms of control, this means
knowing which elements of a situation can be controlled
and which cannot; having identified them, we can adapt to
or work around the uncontrollable and focus more attention on what *can* be controlled. In terms of surrender, accepting reality is itself a preliminary surrender that puts us
in a better position to choose whether further surrender
is our most fruitful option. It gives us a sense of what, if
anything, the object of our surrender will be.

  Each of us is capable of both controlling and surrendering. If we can recognize the way we usually deal with life,
we'll know better whether we need to develop greater abilities to control or to delve more deeply into surrender. Let's
begin by examining self-control.

3 HOLDING THE LINE: SELF-CONTROL

To master others takes force. To master self takes courage.

—Tao te Ching

Who is a powerful man? He who can control himself.

—Talmud

Vidal Sassoon was once asked by an interviewer what it was that enabled him to emerge from the slums of London's East End and become an international celebrity on the beauty and fashion scene. He replied, "I came from a very disciplined background." When I asked him to comment on this further, he said, "I remember at fourteen having to be there in the morning at 8:15 to clean the floors and then at 8:45 to take care of the ladies—there were no charladies, this was wartime England, 1942. I always remember that kind of discipline. . . . I can remember not being the best runner in the school by far, but, by an absolute persistence of training, winning the school championship. . . . I think discipline is a kind of in-depth sense of the way you have to do things. It's part of your character." Later in life, as the owner of an international conglomerate of beauty products, he exercised that same capacity for self-control in determining when he would sell to a larger corporation the company he had developed. "If you have a strong point of reference about your work and you know that it is essentially doing something for the community, those values must never be surrendered. . . . You listen to all the experts out there and they tell you how it's done. And then you turn around and say, 'No. This is the way it will be done. This is me. This is what I'm selling.' It takes enormous self-control. I sense that this goes with the kind of individual we are talking about: the discipline to do it a certain way, the situation where you will not bargain."

Self-control distinguishes the success from the failure, the civilized person from the primitive, the sane from the mad. Without it, society could not exist.

"The major advantage of my ability to control myself is having a chance to accomplish the things I want to in the world around me—and still keep my peace of mind," says Harvey Harrison, an attorney who became a literary agent and who now heads the marketing division of a television production company. Because high-pressure situations are those in which one is most likely to lose control, the ability to maintain self-control in all circumstances is considered a virtue, a sign of leadership. Provided it comes from choice and personal power, its benefits are tremendous. When we have self-control, we feel confident, powerful, able to get things done, and unafraid of the unknown. "Feeling in control of myself and my time has made me able to let myself get a little off course now and then because I know I can get back on. To me that flexibility is an important part of self-control," states Karen Harvey of Now Seminars. The confidence which comes from being sure that we are able to meet our goals and regulate our behavior is priceless. True self-control gives us freedom.

SELF-CONTROL MEANS CHOICE

What is self-control? It is choosing whether or not to act. A young businessman says it's "walking past the chocolate-chip cookies and not eating them"; a psychotherapist says it's "keeping my ego out of the way"; and an eminent diplomat says it's "focusing intelligently on the job at hand." For most of us, having self-control implies *not* doing something (be it eating, drinking, or thinking) we would have done otherwise. However, it is much more than a negative or restrictive force. It means taking possession of our natural faculty for control and accepting the possibility that we have more control than we'd previously believed. It also means we don't have to grab for more or flaunt what we have. Self-control is the hallmark of those with mastery and power.

From the point of view of the object self, it can also be part of us bartering with another for control over our behavior. The laggard in us wants to spend another hour (or two) in bed, and the worker in us wants to hop up and finish all the projects on our desk. They may compromise (laziness on Saturday and work on Monday), or one may dominate for a while (the lazy aspect wins until we run out of money; the worker wins until we drop from exhaustion). For the observer in us, self-control is consciously choosing to do whatever is necessary to produce our intended result. We could also say that it is the ability to accomplish what we want within a set time period without inner struggle. There are no absolutes about applying self-control. Sometimes it's best to use it, and sometimes it's best to lose it.

"I was very angry at my friend, but I decided that I was not going to ruin the relationship by calling her up and spouting off when I was so upset. I deliberately refrained from calling her for several days until I could tell her calmly and directly what was bothering me," said Dana. Self-control helped here. It enables us to set goals and complete projects, tempers potentially destructive urges, and contributes to social stability. Who could give a dinner party if all the guests said exactly what they thought? Self-control gives us a sense of power and choice in an otherwise chaotic world. The tides of the universe may elude our control, but we can at least control ourselves.

Self-control is the ability to *choose* whether or not to act on our impulses. In a sense, it is like a riverbank or a dam. Without banks, a river would be nothing but a broad, flat puddle; confine it and it becomes a powerful channel. Add a dam, and the river becomes a useful source of hydro-electric power. By channeling and even sometimes damming up our personal power, we gain through self-control the power to act—or not act.

WHAT IS IT WE'RE TRYING TO CONTROL?

"I was in a fancy restaurant with my girlfriend a few weeks ago; we were sitting at the bar waiting for our table," says George, a burly ex-college-football player. "I went to the bathroom and when I came out I saw two slick lawyers trying to hustle my girlfriend. They were drunk and were starting to get very obnoxious. Even after I sat down next to her, they kept leaning over to talk to her. She had already asked them to leave her alone; I asked them again. But they thought they were so important that they didn't have to listen, so they kept talking, getting cruder all the time. I really wanted to hit them. The maître d' led us to our table before they pushed me too far, but it took me half the meal to forget about that desire to haul off and sock them."

Physical action is blatant; its control or suppression is

obvious. But our thoughts and feelings, invisible as they are, play a larger role in our behavior, since they precede and usually cause our actions. We are trained from earliest childhood to control our physical impulses. Thoughts and feelings are much more difficult to control than actions; our "control" of them usually amounts to little more than denial or refusal to act them out.

We are in control of ourselves as long as no passion arises that is too strong, as long as our brain and nervous system are functioning properly and we have taken no mind-altering drugs, and as long as we are conscious of the aspects of ourselves that we are trying to control. But how much control is that? Do we have control over when we are born? Or when we die? Or when the people we love will die? No. In more situations than most of us would care to admit, we have absolutely no control at all. That's one reason why self-control is so important—in the few circumstances in which we *can* exercise control, we must do it as well as possible.

We can do much more than we think we can by taking possession of our true capacities for self-control—yet that includes accepting the limits to control. Whether we choose to trade off one behavior for another and call that the best self-control we can get, or harness every shred of energy within us and apply it to meet a goal, our knowledge of ourselves and our willingness to use the control we have give us the power to make things happen.

THE STRESS OF NEEDING CONTROL

"I felt like I was dying. It was as though a vise was closing in on my head—I could hardly breathe," says Roberta, an assistant operations supervisor at a bank. She had just been told that, after she had spent eight years grooming herself to become a district operations supervisor, the job was being eliminated. Always efficient and well organized, she had tried to make sure that nothing came between her and her control. "Forces completely beyond me had stepped in and ruined my plans. My husband's death a few years ago was the first big shock, and then this—I felt like my whole world was collapsing around me. I couldn't cope with anything for weeks. The following month I started having chronic migraine headaches."

Too much or too little control—over ourselves or our circumstances—is stressful and potentially dangerous to our health. If we feel that we have little control or if we need to fill insatiable desires for more control, we are prone to develop stress-related diseases.

As Hans Selye, the pioneer of stress research, points out in *Stress without Distress*,[1] "Stress is the nonspecific response of the body to any demand made on it," whether that demand is something that causes pleasure or pain. According to Selye, "Complete freedom from stress is death." Even jellyfish need a little stress to keep them moving. But while some stress is essential to maintain vitality and enthusiasm, too much or too debilitating stress creates measurable negative effects.

The body has only two basic responses to stress: It learns to live with it or tries to eliminate it. If it decides on elimination, the two options are "fight or flight"; either we try to destroy the cause of our unhappiness, or we run away from it. In contemporary times, neither fight nor flight works very well. If we fight physically, we could get arrested (unless people have bought tickets to watch us), and it's tough to get that warm glow of triumph out of mental fights. When a prehistoric man stood gleefully over the carcass of a mastodon, he *knew* who was boss. We don't get to do that. As for flight, where is there to go?

If we feel we're out of control at our job, we can fight

back by complaining or doing shoddy work, or we can flee by quitting. Both possibilities raise the specter of something even more unpleasant than feeling out of control—being out of a job. Faced with options like this, we tend to keep our feelings and our stresses to ourselves. At least we think we do. Research studies have repeatedly shown that stress predisposes us to high blood cholesterol, high blood pressure, and heart disease, and that the person who needs too much control or who feels he has too little is particularly prone to suffer the many forms of sickness associated with excessive stress.

A *Time* story on stress in July 1983 reported that the vocational groups with the highest incidence of stress-related illness were composed of people who had little sense of control over what happened to them at work. The same issue of *Time* cited earlier reports that a study by Robert Karasek of Columbia University concluded: "People with little control over their jobs, such as cooks and assembly-line workers, have higher rates of heart disease than people who can dictate the pace and style of their work." Within corporations, middle management seems to suffer more stress than highly paid executives who feel that they are in charge of their own destinies.

Whether it's the go-get'em executive or the silently suffering directory assistance operator, both experience the physical and mental effects of debilitating stress because they feel they have less control over their lives than they want. And even the positive stress of challenges to be met and overcome can become unhealthy if it is powered by a relentless struggle for more and more control.

Note that struggling for control is not necessarily related to *having* control and that the stress comes from the struggle. Even those who don't want control often get it if they're good at their work. Trying too hard, needing to do more and more in less time, and needing to control more than is possible may produce some tangible rewards, but they are rewards that might just as easily have been gained with far less stress and at a much lower cost to our health.

Contrary to the beliefs of those who try to hold on when they ought to let go, productivity and efficiency are just as likely to go up as down when the desire for control is relaxed. As Jay Olins, president of California Student Loan Finance Corporation, said to me, "Studies show that people will work harder when they are happy, when they work for people whom they respect and who respect them." We seldom feel respected by people who are trying to control us. This doesn't mean that managers shouldn't be in control. But by *not* making employees feel put upon or overcontrolled, they reduce employee stress—and probably increase productivity. By acting less controlling they actually gain *more* control.

WHEN IS SELF-CONTROL NOT SELF-CONTROL?

"I'm on the windowsill," Myron Goodman reportedly screamed into the telephone, threatening to jump. According to the *Wall Street Journal* (December 31, 1982), Goodman warned his attorney, Joseph L. Hutner, senior partner of the law firm of Singer Hutner Levine & Seeman, that if he did not stop pressuring him to disclose details of a series of frauds he had committed, he would fling himself out the ninth-story window. The *Journal* said that, according to court documents, "Mr. Goodman, shortly after he made the threat, informed a subordinate who had overheard the commotion that it was designed to 'keep the lawyers in their place.'" Throughout the buildup of the fraud, which involved repeatedly bilking major lenders by

drawing up leases for nonexistent or undervalued com-
puters, Goodman periodically broke down and "confessed"
to his attorneys, whom he had drawn as unwitting ac-
complices into his crime. He implied to them that he was
sorry and that his misdeeds were all behind him. They
believed him, continued to represent him, and later discovered that he had continued to write the fraudulent
leases for eight months after his initial "confession." When
he was finally informed that a federal grand jury was issu-
ing subpoenas concerning his company, the *Journal* reported that "according to his own testimony, Mr. Goodman
almost fainted." It was probably the first sincere emotion
he'd shown.

Sometimes it's hard to tell what is self-control and what
isn't because the same behavior can indicate tremendous
self-control, no self-control, or self-suppression. Apparent
lack of control can in fact indicate tremendous presence
of control. The ability to feign a loss of control was used
by Goodman to deceive. It's used by actors to entertain.
It can be used by any petty manipulator to help get something that's desired (as in bursting into tears when our boss
says we'll have to postpone our vacation). And it can even
keep us from getting hurt. Several years ago a football star
and his wife were accosted by a potential attacker. Before
the halfback was able to resort to physical force (which
may or may not have worked) his wife grimaced, grabbed
her buttocks, and yelled, "Oh, God! I'm having a diarrhea
attack!" Not wanting to sully himself on such a smelly
victim, the thug fled.

By the same token, apparent presence of control can
actually result from a compulsive *lack* of control. "Sometimes I hear people praise someone for his great self-
control and I say, 'He doesn't have control—he never
had any feelings to start with!' " says a prominent businessman. Every infant has very strong feelings and no

reservations about expressing them, so it's hard to believe that an adult would truly have "no feelings to start with." But if those feelings are smothered by repression, then the person who appears so stoic, so stable, so controlled, is actually out of all control because he has lost the capacity to choose his response. He cannot choose to withhold the expression of a particular feeling, because he has, for the moment, lost the ability to feel. The apparently raving lunatic can be shrewdly self-controlled and the rock of stability can be choicelessly compulsive.

FINDING THE BALANCE:
FOUR FACTORS TO WATCH FOR

Just as underdeveloped self-control makes us like whimpering babies, excessive self-control kills our vitality—and often prevents us from acting in our own best interests. Finding a balance between the two extremes is what keeps us alive and moving. But how do we find it, and how do we know when we have it? We can feel confident that we're functioning with healthy, life-sustaining self-control if all these factors are positive:

1—*Results*
2—*Appropriateness*
3—*Frame of mind*
4—*Sense of well-being*

1—*Results.* Results, of course, are what actually happen after we act. When we do things that don't work we usually feel worse (an unpleasant result). If our unworkable actions touch the lives of other people, they often feel worse, too. Thus, one way to determine the efficacy of what we did is by referring to how we and those close to us feel, both

immediately afterward and in the long haul. Another way is
to see whether the job at hand was done. If your assistant
is careless about updating appointments in your calendar
and you are so restrained in criticizing him that he thinks
it's not really important, the result may be that you'll miss
a crucial appointment because he cavalierly left it out of
your book. Another example: Your wife asks you what's
wrong and you say, "Nothing," and she comes back with,
"Are you sure?" You might think to yourself, "She wouldn't
understand anyway, so I'll keep my mouth shut," and so
you tell her, "Really, I'm fine." She looks puzzled, hurt,
and slightly angry as she leaves the room. You feel smaller
and somehow more isolated. The results of your tongue
biting were poor.

In the first case, it would have been better if your assistant had come to clearly understand the importance of his
job as a result of your criticism and had therefore jotted
down those appointments with alacrity. At home, a better
result would have been the creation of a sense of warmth
and closeness with your wife, a mutual sense of being
known, understood, and trusted. You might have ended
up with a pleasant conversation instead of a strained silence.

2—*Appropriateness.* Appropriateness is a notoriously
subjective term, yet we all have a sense of what it means.
According to *The Random House Dictionary, appropriate*
is defined as "suitable or fitting for a particular purpose,
person, occasion, etc." It implies recognizing what "fits"
in a given moment and choosing behavior to fit the needs
of that moment. To act appropriately, we must be sensitive
to our surroundings and be capable of choosing the most
apt behavior for ourselves. If we're overly committed to
controlling our environment (whether people, places, or
things), we'll be unable to perceive it clearly enough to
know exactly what's appropriate.

3—Frame of Mind. The frame of mind with which we practice self-control clearly distinguishes self-control from both suppression and indulgence. If a friend keeps every lunch appointment and turns in every work project on time, you might admire her self-control and discipline. But if you then discover that she feels her sense of worth and lovableness depends on her keeping these agreements and that she always feels suppressed and resentful in relationships with friends and employers, would her behavior still seem admirable? Or would it then seem pathetically obsessive? Although she produces impressive results, we could say that she has no self-control at all and is in fact a slave of her own behavior patterns. She does control her behavior well (in that she works at specific projects instead of throwing chewing gum on the ceiling), but her control has a machinelike, rather than a vital, quality.

4—Sense of Well-Being. Well-being is the final, encompassing factor. Both our own well-being and that of those around us measure the combined influence of results, appropriateness, and frame of mind. Having a sense of well-being doesn't necessarily mean feeling happy, or satisfied, or even well rested. A runner completing a marathon may feel exhausted, with bleeding feet and aching legs, but he'll probably have a sense of well-being. A person on a hunger strike for a cause he fully believes in will surely not feel physically satisfied, yet he may have a profound sense of well-being. A mother in labor is in excruciating pain, yet her joy at the birth of her child leaves her flushed with awe and well-being. Someone discharging a duty that he dislikes but considers to be a moral obligation may not feel thrilled, but he may have a sense of well-being. We don't have to feel good to have a sense of well-being.

In fact, although we'd often like to think otherwise, having a sense of well-being has nothing to do with the circumstances of our lives—whether we do or don't have money, food, companionship, or a great sex life. Hermits or spiritual teachers who had none of the "right" circumstances have been hounded for centuries by people who "had it all" but were searching for that elusive feeling of well-being. That's what makes well-being such a great indicator of true self-control: To the person who will sit still for a moment and look inside, its presence or absence is clear. Ask yourself, "Do I have a sense of well-being now?" Poised on the brink of a new or a habitual activity (a job, living with someone, eating a favorite food, visiting a favorite restaurant), ask again, "Does this contribute to my sense of well-being?" The answer springs up instantly, whether we like it or not. If the situation is one that really requires self-control, and the control we're applying is life sustaining, the answer to the question will be a resounding "Yes."

Well-being is in fact a kind of "inner result." If we are producing tremendous outer results through our self-control—profits up, projects completed on time, every second of our day productively used—but we feel chronically tense and oppressed, then we are producing poor inner results in the form of diminished well-being. By continually weighing and balancing the factors of well-being and results, we can avoid the pitfalls of either being very productive and feeling terrible, or feeling great and getting nothing done. Dynamic equilibrium is the key.

Fear-based self-control breaks under pressure; true self-control bends. Desired results, appropriateness, positive frame of mind and sense of well-being are all present when self-control *is* self-control. By observing whether we have all four, and focusing on increasing them, we can gradually diminish the fearful, choking control in our lives and apply the positive control that expands our ability to live.

4 THE UNBREAKABLE MASK: FEAR OF LOSING CONTROL

In January 1983, *Los Angeles* magazine featured an article about Norman Garey, one of the most powerful lawyers in Hollywood. His clients included Marlon Brando, Tony Curtis, and Gene Hackman; he was admired by friends and clients alike for his cool and his self-control. A friend said, "He liked having an effect on people, being in control." Those who knew him were awed not only by his capacity to negotiate multimillion-dollar deals with the shrewdest minds in the entertainment world but by his self-contained attitude. He made his job seem effortless. Garey was so well controlled, in fact, that only his family knew about his struggle with depression and his growing dependence on psychiatric medication. Struggling with the relentless stress of life in the Hollywood fast lane, Garey found it more and more difficult to keep himself in control—yet he could not allow himself to lose it. He went sailing with friends but could not relax or confide in anyone. Finally he was caught in a deadlocked negotiation—his opponent refused to budge on several major points, and Garey faced the possibility of losing a lot of status and a lot of money. Depressed, desperate, but still "in control," he shot himself in the head with a .38-caliber Smith and Wesson revolver. After his death a friend said, "Norman was not walking around like a crazy man. He didn't exhibit signs of depression. He was always the model of organization, awareness, and control."

The fear of losing control traps many of us in an armor of our own making. It is a pervasive and costly fear that robs us of our ability to be flexible and to adapt. We've already established that a certain amount of control over ourselves and our surroundings is beneficial and that too much or too little of it is unhealthy. Now let's look at the primary reason that those of us who are overcontrolled stay that way: *We are afraid of losing control.*

We fear tigers because we don't want claw marks all over our bodies. We fear dark water because we're afraid we'll drown in it. What do we fear might happen if we lost control?

I asked a diverse group of people to complete the sentence "If I lost control . . ." and got an astonishing variety of responses:

A computer engineer: "Everyone would find out what a nasty person I am and they wouldn't like me."

An office boy in a law firm: "I'd get a rifle and blow away everybody in this lousy place."

A lawyer: "I would die."

A psychotherapist: "Nothing would happen if I lost control."

A screenwriter: "I would recover it."

A professional athlete: "I'd do something stupid and embarrass myself."

A free-lance writer: "I wish I could lose control."

A physician: "Who would hold the world together if I did?"

A television executive: "I'd have lost something that wasn't very valuable to me anyway."

A magazine columnist: "I'd eat everything that didn't move."

Most of us feel we have something to lose if we give up self-control. If we try to deal with all our emotional or violent impulses by controlling rather than confronting them, however, those impulses become stronger and more difficult to control. Nearly everybody has something he feels he should hide—some unpleasant or socially unacceptable tendency to be kept under control. Sometimes, as with the boy who'd like to speed his office mates on to their next incarnation, the fear of losing control is justified: If we're going to hurt ourselves or anyone else by losing control, we should be sure *not* to lose control. However, the fear of losing control often becomes a confining motivation *in itself*.

This fear is usually concealed from conscious awareness by two levels of resistance: first, resistance to experiencing the absence of control; second, unwillingness to admit the fear of not being fully in control. There's something embarrassing about admitting that we're afraid of losing control; it gives the lie to our pretense of having been fully in control in the first place. Yet until we can experience and accept the wave of powerlessness that we fear will sweep us to our death, we will avoid losing control as though losing it were losing life itself.

WHERE DOES THIS FEAR
COME FROM?

The fear of losing control is rooted in lack of trust—in ourselves and the world around us. This lack of trust permeates our unconscious attitude and breeds fear, which we then consider to be a realistic reaction to the world around us. Successful people know that examining their fears helps them recover their basic trust and enables them to *choose* their response instead of reacting automatically to the promptings of their unconscious fears.

Another element of this fear is that losing control feels like a return to chaos. Losing control in small ways reminds us that over the fundamentals of life we have no control at all. For some of us, losing control unmasks us and reminds us of our past as helpless infants. For others, it evokes the most primitive fear of death.

The fear of losing control is related to hidden beliefs about having—and not having—control. Our beliefs are generally based on something someone told us or on what happened (or what we think happened) in the past. Neither source is particularly reliable. The people who told us about the world—perhaps our parents or teachers—may have been repeating the fears and misperceptions others conveyed to them. If we could fully experience events for ourselves, without blinders of fear, we might see the universe as a more benign place to live in. As for using the past as a guide to the present, Paul Valéry wrote, "History is the science of what never happens twice."

When we distrust ourselves as reliable or deserving persons and doubt that comfort, order, and support exist in the world, we fear losing control. By seeing that our fear has more to do with lack of trust than with the real consequences of losing control, we begin to develop compassion for the parts of ourselves that block us from trusting. We can then be more pragmatic in our choices about keeping and losing control.

"If only he'd let himself float, he wouldn't have died," said Steven of his high-school friend. Barry had been skindiving near a sewage plant at the local beach. Venturing too close to the intake pipe, he'd been sucked in a flood of seawater into the pipe. He struggled against the violent pull of the water until he died, not from being mangled in machinery, but from exhaustion. "There's a flotation tank in all those plants," sighed Steven. "If he hadn't struggled, he would have floated unharmed to the top." Like Barry, most of us don't know or don't believe that anything but struggle will result in our survival. Sometimes this is true, but often it is not. As long as we are paralyzed by our fear of losing control, we'll never know when to struggle and when to float.

"I DIDN'T KNOW I THOUGHT THAT!"

Paul, the president of a textile-manufacturing company, was faced with a difficult situation. He had to get a mailing out to all his customers, and his entire staff was already busy handling incoming orders. After mulling it over, he hit on what seemed to be the perfect solution. It was summertime, and everyone's children were on vacation. Why not bring in all the kids for an afternoon, give them a few dollars an hour and all the doughnuts they could eat, and let them stuff the envelopes? Everyone was excited about the idea except the director of personnel. She confronted him in the presence of several employees and recited a litany of requirements: They had to be paid minimum wage, they needed tables and chairs, they couldn't sit outside, they had to fill out applications. . . . The enthusiasm drained from the room. The only alternative, said the director, was to get a letter from the chairman of the board authorizing this unusual project. "For a moment I forgot myself," remarked Paul, "and very sternly I said, 'We'll do it this way because I say so!' Of course she was embarrassed in front of everyone. Now I have to find a way to make it up to her so she'll cooperate with me in the future. It was just an instinctive reaction to her challenge to my authority."

It would have been easy enough for Paul to go to the chairman, get the letter, and have the kids come in and work just as he wanted, but his unwillingness to experience a minor loss of control in public created a situation in which he lost control over a key employee (by losing her goodwill). Many thoughts may have flitted through his mind the instant before he responded to her. "I'm the president, how dare she challenge me," and who knows what else. Probably he himself doesn't know. They all added up to his acting on that impulse to challenge her.

We can deduce our hidden beliefs by observing the recurring patterns of our behavior. When considering a beautiful or pleasurable experience, for example, do you tend to think, "Oh, no, I can't have that." Why not? Estelle, an advertising copywriter says, "I used to wonder why everybody else seemed to be having fun while I was missing out. Then I realized that every time someone invited me on a really exciting outing, like snorkeling or going for a picnic, the thought 'I can't go, I have to work' automatically came to mind. I hadn't noticed that I was continually *telling* myself that I wasn't 'allowed' to have fun!"

One way to take a look at our underlying attitudes is to ask ourselves questions like the following:

- Is it always better to control myself? If not, how do I know when it's better and when it's not?

- When is the urge to control myself a function of my best possible self, and when is it a product of my fears, previous conditioning, and peer pressure? How can I tell the difference? (Much of what we pride ourselves on as our great self-control may actually be fear of taking a chance.)

- When I say "I'm afraid of losing control of myself," what do I mean? What *would* happen if I lost control?

As you ask yourself these questions, let the responses come to your mind unimpeded. They're only thoughts, after all. They will gain control over your behavior only if you refuse to think them.

OVERCOMING THE FEAR OF LOSING CONTROL

John, a highly successful businessman in New Jersey, had so dreaded losing his hold on himself that he avoided any situation that might lead him to feel the slightest bit out of control. He refused to drink, use intoxicants of any other sort, or to relax even while playing with his children or making love with his wife. Ever on guard against whatever it was he thought would roar out of him if he let go, John was ruled by his fear of losing control. Not until tragedy hit his family did he begin to break free of his bonds. One of his children was in a serious car accident. Looking at his son's comatose form in the hospital bed, John suddenly lost control of all the emotions he'd been hiding for years. He collapsed in tears in the hospital room and had to be led out by several nurses. Afterward, he could hardly believe he had shown such emotion, but, as he said to his wife, "I feel somehow more relaxed, more at peace. It doesn't make sense to me."

The boy lived, and John found his relationships with all his children and with his wife transformed. His love was no longer locked behind a wall of frozen denial. By letting go, even momentarily, of his resistance to losing control, John actually ended up being less controlled by his fear and more in control of himself.

Nathaniel Branden, author of *Honoring the Self* and numerous other books on psychology and relationships, spoke with me at his Beverly Hills home. He pointed out that many people who feel that they must be in control are controlled by that very need: "In doing therapy with such people, I get them into psychological exercises which show them that they are terrified of being out of control, as the first step in their giving it up. I then get them to make contact with how exhausting it is always to have to be in control. When they are willing to admit how exhausting it is, then it is possible to alter the situation."

Losing control is not always the best course, but the *fear* of losing control blinds us and renders us incapable of choosing whether to keep or let go of control. That's why facing our fear is so important. The more we resist losing control, the more difficult it is to maintain. However, the more we can accept the events and the parts of ourselves we can never control, the more we will be able to master what we can. When we use control consciously—not compulsively, from a need to *not* be out of control—we can enjoy some of its many benefits: goals met, friendships retained, weight not gained.

When we fear losing control of our "selves," it's generally our "dark" impulses we don't want to lose our grip on. (Did you ever hear of someone who dreaded losing control of his kindliness?) Jung called these dark impulses the "shadow" aspect of our personalities: all the uncivilized and potentially destructive tendencies that we find difficult to integrate into our preferred image of ourselves. But the shadow is not evil or destructive in itself. Dr. Ernest Rossi, a Jungian analyst in Brentwood, California, and the author of numerous books on dream psychology and hypnosis, told me, "The shadow is a secret emissary of the self, a secret freedom fighter. It is dark only to the extent that we have been dark to our inner nature. If we ignore our inner nature, this shadow begins to get feisty, because it is fighting for our inner needs." That is, it becomes destructive only if we suppress it. By denying the "shadow" aspects of ourselves, we lock them behind a door of willpower and control—from which they *must* eventually escape.

We often cling to control because we do not trust that anything good will come, either from ourselves or from the world, unless we are always working to make things turn out our way. The hardest part of giving up the fear of losing control is learning to trust—at least trust the possibility—that there is goodness in our natures and order in the universe, and that they will show up if we will let go of our fear and give them a chance.

A SEVEN-STEP PROCESS FOR OVERCOMING THE FEAR OF LOSING CONTROL

The person who lacks self-control is unable to move beyond the distractions of the moment. Yet the person who cannot give up control is a machine. When we feel we *must* always be in control of ourselves, we are addicts, helpless victims of our compulsion to control. We may even recognize that we need to lose control, and long for a breathing moment of freedom from our inner confines, yet feel utterly incapable of letting go. We must learn to *deal* with the fear of losing control if we want to function freely. The following seven steps will help:

1—*Notice that you have the fear.* Before we can get rid of it, we must know that we have it. It's like the prince who had a papaya-shaped wart on the side of his nose. His father never let anyone show him a mirror, so he believed he was the handsomest man in the world. One day he was trying to seduce a young beauty and she pulled away from him, saying, "How can I kiss a man with a wart like that?" Said the prince, "Wart? What wart?" We all have a bit of that prince inside us saying, "Fear? What fear?"

Many of us use certain phrases, such as "I'm not sure that's a good idea" or "That's just not the kind of thing I do," or take particular body postures (arms folded, abdominal muscles suddenly clenched, and so forth) when what we are really expressing is "I'm afraid of losing control." What are *your* personal signs of the fear of losing control?

2—*Accept that you have the fear.* Although this sounds simple, it can be very difficult in practice. Most of us have strong opinions about ourselves that we would like to believe are correct. Being afraid of losing control may not fit our idealized self-image, so accepting the presence of such a powerful fear may require us to set aside years of defensiveness and conditioning. A good way to begin is to remember that nearly everybody has it. You are not alone. Having a fear does not mean you are a bad person or a lesser person. It doesn't even mean that you will always act on the fear. It just means that you have it.

3—*Imagine losing control.* I asked a San Francisco poet what would happen if she lost control. She said, "My initial reaction was 'Control? What's that? Who's in control, for heaven's sake?' Only later I had to admit that that was a lie. Even though I make a grand show as a creature of impulse, I am terrified of losing control." By imagining what would happen if she lost it, she saw how important control was in her life.

What would happen if you lost control? How would it feel, look, or smell if you lost control? Feel it in your body, see it in your mind. You don't actually have to lose control to imagine what it would be like. The next time someone, say, invites you unexpectedly to a party, notice whether that resistance inside comes from a realistic appraisal of the new option or from fear of not being in control of your environment, schedule, and companions.

4—*Fully experience the fear in your body.* This exercise will carry you deeper into overcoming this fear. Lie down in a safe, comfortable place, wearing loose clothing. Imagine losing control, or evoke the fear of losing control within you, and let it wash through your body. You may find yourself shaking violently, crying, shouting "No," or experiencing totally unexpected reactions. Let them happen. They will subside on their own. You may have to practice this over a series of days or weeks until finally nothing much happens when you invite the fear to come forward.

Some people might need the assistance of a psychotherapist, hypnotherapist, or skilled body worker to help them bring this fear to light. If you feel apprehensive about doing it yourself, find a qualified professional to help you.

5—*Imagine the worst thing that could happen if you lost control.* Create a "worst case" scenario and see how awful it would be. Would you really eat an elephant if you lost control? Usually the consequences would not be as shattering as we'd feared.

6—If you really can't afford to be out of control, then *visualize yourself being in control.* The fear of losing control may be precisely the thing that keeps us *out* of control. Stage fright is a common example. A nervous actor may be so terrified of losing control of himself and forgetting his lines while on stage that he can frighten himself into doing just that. By visualizing the whole performance going flawlessly (and rehearsing a lot), he can be confident of staying in character and in control. Taking tests is also a common way of bringing out our fear of losing control. One attorney recalls that when she faced the ordeal of the California State Bar exam, she continually visualized what she would do after successfully completing it. "I saw myself leaving the examination room, throwing away the pencils and pens I'd used, and then going to celebrate with my friends," she says. While she certainly had prepared herself in other ways, she did pass the test the first time and acted out her fantasy just as she'd imagined it.

7—*Take a chance.* If someone offers to take you hot-air ballooning and the fearful controller in you screams, "What!? You'll fall!"—stop. Take a deep breath. Look and see if doing this would really damage you or if you are really just afraid of being out of control. If it's the latter, then let the fear be there and take it along for the ride. If you still want to refuse, then tell the person who invited you the real reason why: "I'd love to, but I'm afraid of losing control."

We can also, in safe places and without hurting anyone, *practice* losing control in small ways so that we can face our fears bit by bit. If, to you, losing control is dancing naked around the living room and you're timid about it, then take a Sunday afternoon or an evening, close the shades, and do the rites of Spring. Who really cares if you do? And why should you care if they care? Just notice whatever fears arise around that little freedom and let them be felt. Then dance.

OVERCOMING FEAR THROUGH ACCEPTANCE

Until we befriend the unconscious life that seems chaotic to our conscious mind, we will be unable to choose whether or not to have self-control. Our fear of losing control does its job for a while, keeping mystery and chaos out of sight, but if it does its job too well it also obliterates our love, compassion, and creativity. Moreover, the fact is that if we're trying to get through life on the strength of our control, we'll never be able to control enough. We can't keep it up forever. Eventually the dam of control cracks and our worst fears come true: We really do lose control—in an uncontrolled flood rather than a modulated stream.

The keys to overcoming the fear of losing control are simple. If we trust ourselves to know when to pull back in case we start to let go more than is beneficial and appropriate, then we can afford to let go. If we learn to stop and breathe before we lunge into action, we can choose to act with self-control. By developing self-confidence and the ability to shift into the observing mode of mind and *choose*, we go beyond our ordinary barriers and behave appropriately and freely.

5 *"I'VE GOT TO CONTROL MYSELF!": BUT HOW?*

The late Tommy Thompson, best-selling author of *Blood and Money, Serpentine,* and *Celebrity,* was a guest speaker at a private writing seminar I once attended in the Hollywood Hills. He told us that he got up every morning at the same time and at 8:00 A.M. sat at his desk—shaved, dressed, and breakfasted—to work at least until noon. He stuck to this habit for over twenty years. "If I can't think of anything to write one morning," said Thompson, "I'll sit there and retype the previous day's pages until either my writing time is over or the work starts to flow." Multimillionaire Jerry Buss told me in a private interview that he develops self-control by forcing himself to keep to his schedule regardless of what he feels like doing at a particular time. World-class martial arts competitor Darryll Leiman works out daily whether he feels like it or not. People who excel *work* to develop their self-control.

Self-control takes many forms. In the practical world, the capacity to set goals and meet them is one of its valuable and visible forms. Verbal self-control—tact, courtesy, and discretion—makes our relationships flourish. "Developing self-control has meant that I no longer have to regret things I said and did; it's made me more effective in relationships," says Jewish community leader Susan Lapin. Some people find it easier than others to master self-control; some seem to have been born with it. For most of us, however, self-control is learned. Let's look at some of the ways to develop this valuable skill.

Nobody ever got worse at something by practicing it. This is true of self-control, too. The question is, how do we do it?

Before we can apply specific control techniques, we need to look more closely at what it is we're trying to control and why we haven't controlled it yet. "I lost thirty pounds after I stopped trying to control my *weight* and started controlling my *eating*," says Donna Langer, who now counsels those who cannot control their eating. Imagine trying to turn off a hose by stomping on the nozzle instead of turning off the spigot: You'd always be frustrated because you hadn't eliminated the water flow at its source. In the same way, if we try to control the *effects* of what we do instead of the *causes*, we're in for a lot of frustration. Many of us fret about the results of our lack of self-control without delving into its causes. Why?

WE ALREADY HAVE ALL THE SELF-CONTROL WE NEED

It actually takes a lot of self-control to be fat or intoxicated or chronically late. To stay fat, we have to keep ourselves away from appetizingly healthy fruits, vegetables, and grains and from the energizing pleasure of exercise. To be drugged or drunk, we must find and purchase expensive chemicals, frequently at great cost to our career, personal relationships, and financial stability. Even being late requires a certain amount of planning, although it might be unconscious. How many times can we pretend that there will be no traffic, no construction trucks stopped in the middle of the road, no problems parking? Why should a task that took half an hour every other time we've done it suddenly take fifteen minutes? Usually, we know when we're preparing to be late. And we could just as easily say that we disciplined ourselves mightily to prevent ourselves from leaving on time as that we lacked control and therefore were late.

So those who are fat, drunken, tardy layabouts (or any lesser version of same) can take heart: They already have plenty of self-control. They're just applying it to useless ends.

One of the first steps in developing *productive* self-control is to see why we have been applying our great skill at self-control in what are apparently our own worst interests. What are we gaining from this pose of not having self-control? "I developed a serious drug problem out of trying to keep up with my friends who were using a lot of drugs," says Robert, now a (non-drug-abusing) fashion designer in New York. What looked like uncontrolled pill popping was actually a concentrated, if unconscious, effort to seem more "hip" and therefore more acceptable to his addicted friends. "I used to be late to many appointments because I thought it was acceptable for business people to be late," says Karen Harvey. "Then I realized that the later I was, the more I proved to my customers that I could not be relied upon. That cost me business. As I lost more business, I really saw the cost of being late. After that, I realized the importance of time management and I just started planning to be on time." Harvey now teaches a time-management course throughout the country and is writing a book about it in her spare time.

Stop and think for a moment about which areas of life you wish you had more control in—weight, time, exercise, speech. Next, complete the sentence "If only I could stop _____, I would be happier and more productive."

Then take a deep breath and ask yourself, "What am I gaining by continuing to deal with this the way I do?" For
example, we might say, "If only I could stop speaking before
I think, I would be happier and more productive." Then we
would ask, "What am I gaining by what I am doing now?"
and perhaps get an answer such as "I get a lot of attention
from other people." Let the answers spring to mind without
censoring them. (This is an area in which it pays to use zero
control. Let your mind speak to you freely, and it may tell
you the truth before you can say, "Oh, not that. It couldn't
be *that*." Yes, it could.)

After examining the benefits of acting as though we had
no self-control, we can ask ourselves, "What has my lack of
self-control *cost* me in terms of health, well-being, productivity, and satisfaction in my relationships? How much has
it cost me in money and jobs? What has it cost me in self-
respect?" In the case of speaking without thinking, we might
answer, "It's cost me the trust and affection of those closest
to me, ruined relationships with employees and clients,
made me spend inordinate amounts of time and energy
justifying myself," and so on. After comparing the benefits
with the costs, it will probably be clear to you whether the
cost is worth the reward. It may be worth it to you. If the
cost is too high, high enough to make you want to find new
sources of productive behavior within yourself, however,
read on.

SELF-CONTROL: HOW TO GET IT

The following are just a few of the techniques you can use
to enhance your self-control:

   • *Ask yourself what would constitute "having self-
control" for you.* How can we know whether we have self-
control if we're not sure what it is to us? There are some

standards of self-control built into our legal system, covering activities such as drunk driving, drug abuse, physical violence, and pulling flowers from public gardens. In addition to the legal definitions of self-control, each of us has inner pictures of what it would be like to have self-control. How would it look to you? How would you know if you had it? What would it feel like to have self-control, or more self-control than you do now? If you had self-control, would you never again spank your child? Never light another cigarette? Know what standards you're trying to reach.

• *Learn to control the breath.* Meditation masters have known this for millennia, but people from Western cultures have been listening to them seriously for only the past few decades. When we control the breath, we control the mind. And this does not mean holding your breath when you get mad.

The instinctive reaction to fearful circumstances is to begin breathing shallowly, from the upper chest rather than the diaphragm and abdomen. When we're excited (or frightened), whether by scary tigers or alluring tigresses, we naturally start to breathe faster. In the midst of this excitement, pleasant or unpleasant, we get a little jumpy. And sometimes we act on impulse, without forethought or fore–anything else. We don't always use self-control. Body and mind may get out of sync. The mind races ahead, conjuring up imaginary monsters down the track, or the body plunges into soon-to-be-regretted action. When we get excited, we often lose control.

We regain control by controlling the breath. To do this, we begin by noticing how we are breathing, how much of our chest is being filled by each breath, and then by consciously overriding those shallow little sniffs and taking a series of deep, complete abdominal breaths. Suddenly the situation does not look quite so overpowering.

• *Practice controlling yourself in situations that ordinarily prompt you to lose control.* The medieval Jewish scholar Moses Maimonides recommended that when people are trying to overcome some bad habit, they test themselves by voluntarily putting themselves in situations that upset their self-control. Rabbi Daniel Lapin of Bay Cities Synagogue in Venice, California, gives an example: "If driving in rush-hour traffic makes you insanely angry, then set aside time once a week or so and drive at 5:15 P.M. to the busiest freeway interchange in your city. Drive two miles north, then get off and drive two miles south, all the while monitoring your reactions. You'll probably find that after a few practice sessions you'll be saying 'I've got to find something that really makes me angry. This is boring.' "

• *Write down realistic goals for developing self-control.* For example, you could write, "For me, self-control would look like skipping dessert five times a week." (It could just as well be "jogging three times a week" or something else.) "I will start skipping dessert as of March 15." If you now have two helpings seven nights a week, you might want to start skipping it once or twice a week and work up to your goal.

By writing down your self-control goals, setting dates by which you'll meet them, and referring to them regularly, you bolster your natural capacity for self-control.

• *Get someone else to control you for a while.* Jerome, an independent businessman, was having trouble keeping track of his accounts and found himself inadvertently writing bad checks. He finally gave all his checkbooks to his accountants and instructed them not to let him write checks except on the first and the fifteenth of the month. Within a few months, he was able to take control of his own accounts.

People who are trying to become physically fit often use

this technique, too. They hire a trainer to come to their home early in the morning and pay him good money to haul them out of bed if they're still nestling in the delicious comfort of warm blankets at 6:00 A.M. After a while (so they tell us at parties) they are hopping out of bed at 5:30 to greet their trainer cheerfully at the door.

- *Arrange a support group.* Related to the previous suggestion, this means getting other people to support you in your burgeoning self-control. It's easier for all of us to be disciplined if we get acknowledgment and support from other people for doing it.

That means asking your family to congratulate you when you lose weight or asking your friends to refuse when you ask to bum a cigarette. Having one or more people aligned in support of your personal goals increases the power of your efforts many times over.

- *Congratulate yourself when you show self-control.* Other people will not always know when you have applied self-control, since self-control often means *not* acting. Thus, it's essential that you congratulate yourself when you do it. Pat yourself on the back when you successfully resist temptation or apply yourself with disciplined focus toward reaching a goal.

TRUTH OR CONSEQUENCES

The key to developing more self-control is this: Observe the results of your behavior, controlled or uncontrolled. Once you've developed this habit, it becomes easier to use the technique that transcends all others: Create a "choice point" before every questionable activity. Before opening your mouth or moving, stop and make a choice. "Do I really want to do this?" "I've observed the results of this before—do I want to experience them again?" "Based on other experiences, I can imagine what the results of this action will be. Am I willing to take the consequences?" If you are, and what you're contemplating won't damage anyone else, well . . . either do it or don't. Just be clear that you are *choosing* and that along with choosing the act, you are choosing to be responsible for its effects.

A clear appraisal of the probable results of our actions is even more powerful than willpower. The disciplined eater knows the effects of various foods on his mood and waistline and chooses those that give him the effects he wants. The food addict goes for the quick fix and watches the consequences collect around his thighs. When we have a strong impulse, we can control it, eliminate it, or imagine the probable result and freely choose one *result* over another. So the question is not so much, *"Can* I do this?" or *"Should* I do this?" as it is, "Am I willing to cope with the consequences of this?"

If we use our natural capacity for control, step out of our momentary dilemma, and view the probable results of our actions from the observer's standpoint, we can opt for healthy self-control most of the time. Take a deep breath, consider the consequences, and choose. You have more self-control than you think.

ENOUGH IS ENOUGH: HOW TO SPOT EXCESSIVE SELF-CONTROL

Just as insufficient self-control debilitates us in choosing what we want to do, so does having too much.

"I wish I *could* lose control," says Anne, a free-lance writer in her early thirties. "I'm so bottled up I could scream." Self-control is great, but enough is enough. "My wife keeps telling me she wishes I was less controlled—I never seem to be able to relax and enjoy myself," says George, a computer engineer. While too little self-control inclines us to lie on the beach all day or volunteer for yet another time-wasting committee, excessive self-control may needlessly keep healthy tendencies down. It also shuts us out of many delightfully uncontrolled adventures. Like the man who doesn't feel dressed unless he's wearing a necktie, we can come to consider a choke hold of overcontrol to be normal, and flexibility a threat.

Every time we get a table in a restaurant where no one else could, win back the affections of someone who'd planned to leave us, or leave a competitor stranded, we get a little thrill of power, a sense of another piece of the universe that's become part of our domain. At what point do these thrills become dangerous? When do they become "control fixes" that we crave to affirm our value to ourselves and the world?

If a lot of your friends tell you to your face that you're too controlling, there's probably hope for you. If no one tells you you're too controlling, but people seem anxious, slightly hostile, and strained around you, take heed. It may not be all their problem. When we have to know everything that's going on around us, particularly if we feel we have to take care of every detail around us—like the company president who insists on changing the light bulbs in his office—we probably have an overdeveloped need for control. Do you find it impossible to forget about your work? Are you secretly convinced that the world would fall to pieces if you didn't personally hold it together? Do you always know how other people should run their lives? Are you sure that you are responsible for everyone else's mistakes? Do you always have to have the last word? Do you feel uncomfortable about answering these questions? Then you may well be an overcontrolling person.

Do you frequently experiment with dangerous situations and substances, trying to prove your mastery over them? Anything from race-car driving to drug abuse can indicate an excessive need to control—we try to master the machine to prove that we can turn back just this side of a wreck and to temper our drug intake just this side of all-out addiction. The irony is that while we're trying to prove that we're "in control" of our destinies, we're simultaneously proving that we're addicted to control.

Ask yourself, "Can I let go when there's nothing more I can do about a situation?" "Can I delegate a task to someone I trust and not fret over whether it will be done?" "Am I in love with control?" If you're not sure, ask your spouse, or your secretary, or your coworkers. They know.

An excessive need for control and excessive self-control can take on many virtuous disguises. This is what makes it so difficult to identify. Couldn't the behavior that one person labels "excessively controlling" just as easily be seen as conscientious, responsible behavior? Yes and no. "I'm not trying to *control* him," one might say. "I'm just trying to keep him from making a big mistake." Certainly, attempting to keep things and ourselves "under control" is a sign of social conscience and responsibility, but the *inability to let go* is the key factor that differentiates balance from excess.

BREAKING THE GRIP
OF OVERCONTROL

If you have determined that you are among the many who are hung up on overcontrol, you've already taken a major step toward balance. Most control fanatics don't think they're into control. They believe that their responses are rational and necessary in a disordered and otherwise uncontrolled world. They're not overcontrolled: Everyone else is undisciplined. Like the little boy in the movie *Black Orpheus* who believes that the sun won't rise unless he plays his flute for it at dawn, we think our control is the main force that keeps entropy from overwhelming our orderly world. Questioning this assumption is an essential part of releasing the grip of excessive self-control. So if what you've read in this chapter seems uncomfortably familiar, take heart. Your discomfort is the beginning of your transformation.

There are specific techniques you can use to overcome excessive self-control. Many of them are similar to those used for overcoming the fear of losing control in general. They are intended to help us get rid not of the self-control that brings positive results and well-being but of the many rigid fixations that pass for self-control. The techniques are easy, and most of them can be applied as you go about your daily life:

• *Develop the "pause button" routine.* Most tape recorders have a pause button that can be pushed to interrupt the tape momentarily without shutting off the power. This is a useful option if you're not sure whether the tape you're listening to is one you really want to hear. We can do the same thing with our minds. When a particularly repetitive mental "tape" begins to play ("I can't do that, I have to work, I'm too busy, what will people think, I don't dare . . ."), stop and ask, "Is this control really necessary, or am I trying too hard to hold on?"

• *Imagine what would happen if you let go.* How would it feel? How would it look? What if you lost control, not of everything or for always, but just for this moment, now? If something really unpleasant or damaging to another would result from your loss of control, then hold on. Often, however, what we really fear is not the consequences of our loss of control but the experience of the depth of our fear of letting go.

• *Ask yourself, "What's the worst thing that could happen if I lost control of myself in this situation?"* Everyone has his own "worst case" image of what would happen if he lost control. For some, it includes embarrassment; for others, reduced net worth. When we look at it, the worst case often turns out not to be catastrophic at all. (If losing control really would be catastrophic, don't do it. But make sure that your fears are based in reality.)

• *Notice when you "protest too much"* about your certainty and control. "When I know I've got the answers, I know I'm in trouble," says psychologist Nancy Zapolski. "For me, when I start saying, 'I've got this under control,' 'I've got that handled,' and all that, I always use that as a sign that I'm asleep to something. Because 'keeping the question open' is for me the way of staying open to different possibilities. And when we *know* we're in control and *know* we've got things handled, then we've at the very least limited our possibilities."

• *Give yourself "miniholidays" from control.* One evening a week, or for half an hour or so every day, take a break, a period in which you assume absolutely no responsibility for the problems of the world, and don't care if the sky does fall in. Let yourself relax. Without causing pain to yourself or others, allow yourself to lose control. For example, you could duck out of the office for a half hour in the park or watch a soap opera on television before resuming your household responsibilities. It's the perfect out for an overcontroller; what makes it different from an ordinary binge-out loss of control is that you *know* what you're doing. You are choosing to let go of control.

- *Allow yourself to experience the fear that holds your overcontrol in place.* This is the most powerful technique for overcoming excessive self-control. Fears take root in our bodies and create knots of tension. You can uproot them as you sit at your desk or anywhere you can quietly look within for a few minutes. Take a few deep breaths and "scan" your body with your mind's eye. Try to locate the armored pockets of "I have to be in control," "I'll die if I lose control." A skilled practitioner of deep massage can also help you find the knots deep in your body, but the loosening up begins with your willingness to experience the fear. Even as adults, there may be vulnerable or childlike aspects within us that need comforting. Look beneath the shield of fear and comfort the quivering child inside. It might be all right to lose control. Look and see.

When we hold ourselves too tightly in control, people wonder what we're trying to hide. Overcontrol makes us rigid beams in the shifting structure of reality—and it's not reality that's likely to break first. Options shift, situations shift, and while there may be some principles that we will never alter, the winners in the modern world will be those who can control or let go *by choice* and not through fear.

6 *"WHY DID I DO THAT?"*: *UNCONSCIOUS CONTROL*

It is often tragic to see how blatantly a man bungles his own life and the lives of others yet remains totally incapable of seeing how much the whole tragedy originates in himself, and how he continually feeds it and keeps it going. Not *consciously* of course—for consciously he is engaged in bewailing and cursing a faithless world that recedes further and further into the distance. Rather, it is an unconscious factor which spins the illusions that veil his world. And what is being spun is a cocoon, which in the end will completely envelop him.

—Carl Jung[1]

Martin Hall was sitting in a business meeting, ready to clinch a deal he'd been developing for eight months. His client leaned forward to make a point, and Martin caught a whiff of a distinctive men's cologne that he hadn't smelled in years—not since his stepfather had come at him with a hickory cane after he'd stolen a dollar from his mother's wallet. He couldn't quite recall where he'd smelled that scent before, but a wave of anger swept through him. The client kept smiling and talking about the new line of menswear Martin's company would be manufacturing for him, but Martin was suddenly impatient. "Well, if you really think grown men would want to wear pink suits, I *guess* we could produce them," he said. Taken aback, the client replied, "Well, if that's the way you feel, perhaps we'd better reconsider the whole thing." Afterward, when trying to explain to his boss why the deal was now in jeopardy, Martin kept shaking his head, "I don't know what happened—something just came over me."

Unconscious control occurs when thoughts and feelings of which we are not fully aware run our lives. When we do things, particularly things that are clearly not in our best interest, and we don't know why, we are exhibiting unconscious control. For example, a person may have an unconscious belief that he deserves to fail; if he is not conscious of this but always manages to fail at his endeavors, we can say his life is *unconsciously* controlled by that belief. Usually, the greater the unconsciousness, the greater the dismay. The feelings we keep unconscious are often the ones we'd prefer not to have; denied expression through language and thought, they naturally find expression in potent and mischievous ways.

There's only one way to determine if we're functioning on the basis of unconscious control: observing what we do. When we feel our behavior is "out of control," we're being controlled by forces outside our conscious awareness. The more *willing* we are to become aware of those forces, the more aware of them we will become. Consciousness is easy to reach; it is waiting for us to stop clinging to unconsciousness.

Freud once said, "That which is unconscious results in mischief and unproductive behavior." Jung also felt that the repressed unconscious mind, or "shadow," would lead to trouble if forced out of conscious awareness. Conscious thoughts and beliefs affect us strongly, but our unconscious thoughts and beliefs are even more powerful, since their only expression is through manifestation in the material world. If we are conscious of a conflict, we can talk and think about it objectively, expressing our feelings and gradually working through them. On the other hand, feelings that are suppressed into unconsciousness find expression in powerful, unintended ways. For example, if a man is angry at his wife but does not tell her so, he may "forget" her birthday or begin to make subtly derogatory remarks about her to their children and friends. As long as he denies his anger, it will seep out in nasty but hard-to-pin-down ways. If he continues to express his unconscious feelings in this indirect manner, the entire relationship may be jeopardized.

"I've been working my tail off and I just don't seem to be getting anywhere," complained Sharon, owner of a secretarial service. "I see so many other people who aren't nearly as smart or as efficient as I am making money, and I'm still sweating the rent." Further conversation revealed that Sharon's family was always poor, so she had no role models of people who either knew how to make money or believed they deserved it. Although she was *consciously* set on success, her unconscious beliefs told her that people like her never make it big. "I know it's something in my attitude that's keeping me from doing well, but I don't know exactly what it is or what to do about it," said Sharon. "It's very frustrating." When she becomes fully aware of her unconscious attitude about deserving poverty, she will have taken the first step in overcoming the unconscious control that keeps her poor.

HOW TO RECOGNIZE
UNCONSCIOUS CONTROL

How can we tell if our lives are dominated by unconscious control? If we keep getting what we don't want and it looks like it's not our fault, then we are probably acting out beliefs we're barely aware we have. Other indications of unconscious control include recurring health problems, particularly those that are often psychosomatic, such as headaches, allergies, digestive disorders, and skin rashes. If you feel constantly victimized by others, have a long string of accidents, are plagued by bizarre coincidences, or find yourself harassed by endless streams of fearful, anxious thoughts, there's a good chance that you are manifesting some unconscious attitude or conflict.

Even such common habits as chronic lateness, proscrastination, and obsessive perfectionism can indicate that our motivations are not quite what they seem. What appears to be a character trait may actually point to an unconscious attitude about our willingness or right to succeed. Rather than become aware of the unconscious attitude "I deserve to fail," we may develop a self-image that reinforces the attitude. For example, we might say, "Oh, I'm just a person who has trouble getting things done." The actual *result* of not getting things done is failure in business and relationships; until we see the connection between that conscious thought, its related behavior (never finishing anything), and the unconscious attitude that produced it, we're liable to stay on the treadmill of unconscious control.

It's no crime to have some unconscious attitudes. Nevertheless, we can try to be as conscious as possible as often as possible.

"I can't stand to watch him do it again," said Harold, the close friend of a man who had begun—and bankrupted

—five small newspapers in ten years. "He makes the same mistakes every time. He doesn't get enough capital to start with, makes promises to his investors he knows he can't keep, and ends up losing his shirt—and everyone else's, too. What really kills me is that every time he launches a new paper, he acts as though all the problems of the previous fiascoes were accidents." Particularly when we are unconscious, staying unconscious seems like our safest bet. It feels comfortable in the same way that being under an anesthetic is comfortable: We don't feel the pain. However, the anesthetic is not the cure.

WHERE DOES UNCONSCIOUS CONTROL COME FROM?

"I really want to move ahead in this company," says Arthur, a handsome former professional swimmer. "I understand swimwear and the needs of swimmers, so I'm sure eventually I can become head of marketing." Although he does have the knowledge needed to move ahead in this international sporting goods company, Arthur has a disconcerting tendency to blow opportunities just as they're about to break. En route to a crucial meeting with a supplier, his car (which had needed service for months) breaks down; he is late for a meeting with his immediate boss and the head of the swimwear division; he forgets to bring an essential piece of information to a meeting with his subordinates. After a few years as assistant head of marketing, Arthur is passed over when his boss is promoted. A more reliable person from another company is recruited to be the new head of marketing. Frustrated, Arthur complains, "What's wrong with the management here? Didn't they know I was the perfect candidate for that job?" He does not see that although he consciously believed (and said) that he wanted to advance, his actions belied his words.

Constant frustration in getting what we want often springs from an inconsistency between our conscious desires and our unconscious beliefs. Without first bringing those unconscious beliefs to light, we will find it exceedingly difficult to fulfill our conscious desires.

In *The Psychology of Romantic Love*, Nathaniel Branden points out that parents, without realizing it, often send their children emotionally charged messages that certain of their feelings are bad or wrong. While consciously we might think that "it's all right for me to be happy" or "I deserve pleasure," our unconscious mind, which was powerfully conditioned before we knew what was happening, might disagree. Branden writes: "Thus a child can be led to the conclusion that his feelings are potentially dangerous, that sometimes it is advisable to deny them, that they must be 'controlled.' What such 'control' means practically is that a child learns to *disown* his or her own feelings, effectively ceasing to experience them. . . . In denying feelings, in nullifying his or her judgments and evaluations, in repudiating his or her experience, the child has learned to disown parts of the self, of the personality."[2] These disowned selves often show up by producing "inexplicable" thoughts and behaviors. The manifestations might include feelings of hatred, envy, destructiveness, and self-sabotage; infantile fears of falling and being left alone; irrational angers; and all those things that cool, enlightened grown-ups aren't supposed to have. But have them we do, and to the extent that we deny them, they run our lives. The more we try to repress such thoughts and feelings, the more solidly entrenched they become. We don't seem to realize that we can be conscious of them without acting them out.

All of us are unconscious about something (most of us

are about a lot of things); the more unconscious we are, the more inexplicable problems we have. *Given two conflicting intentions, one conscious and one unconscious, the unconscious one always produces the clearest results.*

If something unwanted—from parking tickets to poverty —comes up again and again in your life, consider the possibility that you're not looking at some underlying cause. (Maybe you should stop parking in red zones.) If you *think* you know why annoyances recur and yet they still persist, then perhaps you don't *really* know why; or there is another, more powerful reason you are overlooking; or some part of you is getting too valuable a payoff from your calamities to let them stop; or your understanding of the reason is so cerebral that it doesn't touch the powerful feelings which actually trigger your behavior. Look again.

TELLING OURSELVES TO SHAPE UP

"As soon as I realized that I was ruining all my relationships with men by finding fault and nagging them until we broke up, I resolved to stop doing that," says Susan. "But it was strange—even though I'd promised myself I'd stop, I found those critical thoughts just creeping into my mind—and I broke up with some really nice guys." A natural tendency when we spot an unconscious pattern that works against our best interests is to wish it weren't there. After all, it's pretty embarrassing to realize that problems were caused not by other people, timing, or the economy but by the fact that at some primitive level of ourselves failure seemed like the only thing to do. After wishing it weren't there, the next tendency is to slap the hand of the unconscious mind and tell it to cut it out. Unfortunately, it is never enough just to decide not to do it again. How many times have you decided never to eat another package of cookies? Or drink too much? Or yell at your kids? The unconscious mind doesn't seem to take orders from the conscious mind on subjects it already thinks it knows how to handle.

Some psychologists claim that the unconscious mind does not understand the concept of "no." Its job is to say "yes, yes, yes" to whatever emotionally charged messages the conscious mind feeds it. Many of these messages are delivered to the unconscious when we are children, incapable of deciding which are true and which are false. Like the rest of us, the unconscious mind likes to be right, and if the emotional instructions we give it are strong enough, it will set up the circumstances to prove its position. For example, if you have a belief that the world is full of knaves who are out to cheat you, every honest person will seem like an exception—even when the honest ones outnumber the dishonest ones ten to one. Moreover, you are more likely to interpret well-intentioned words and acts as covert attempts to cheat you, and you may even manage to attract all the dishonest people in your vicinity into your life in an unconscious attempt to prove that your belief is right. When this happens, your unconscious mind is just doing its job: saying "yes" to its deeply entrenched beliefs.

Many New Year's resolutions fail because the desires of the conscious mind are out of line with the person's unconscious programs (and often with reality). You may *consciously* want to quit smoking, but *unconsciously* consider a cigarette a reward for a job well done; you may *consciously* want to double your income, but *unconsciously* believe you're not worth it. The best New Year's resolution would really be to get in touch with the unconscious resistance that kept all the previous resolutions from working.

WHATEVER WE RESIST, PERSISTS

Whatever we strongly resist comes to us faster than what we strongly want. A father orders his daughter, "Go sit in the corner and *don't* think about pink elephants." What can she think about but those big pink pachyderms? How many times have you set out to specifically avoid running into a particular person, only to end up seated next to him on a bus or at a dinner party? Whether we are resisting people, thoughts, or events, the strength of our resistance projects huge amounts of energy into whatever it is we want to avoid. Our very focus on avoiding what we don't want causes the situation we are resisting to persist. One advantage of this is that continuing to attract our least desirable circumstances gives us repeated opportunities to work out whatever conflicts we have associated with them. Continually bumping into the people and situations that most annoy us may not seem like an advantage, but if we use every episode as an opportunity to find out why this is happening, the repetition works in our best interest. Once we resolve the issue behind the conflict, we don't care much about the conflict either way—and it "magically" ceases to be a recurrent problem in our lives.

For example, Elaine is a lovely woman in her late twenties who has an uncanny penchant for falling in love with married men. For years she followed the axiom that "All the good ones are married"; since she wanted a "good one," only married men got her attention. As her thirtieth birthday approached, she started thinking about getting married herself, and it suddenly seemed like a good idea to date single men. "That's it," she resolved, "from now on I'm only dating single men." Nevertheless, she continued to entangle herself with men who were living with other women or were already involved in relationships.

Finally she met George Phillips, who seemed like the perfect man for her. In his late thirties, he was exciting, sensitive, good-looking, prosperous, and, she thought, completely unattached. She fell for him all the way. Absorbed in fantasies about her upcoming engagement, she overlooked the telltale signs that she would once have noticed immediately—mysterious weekend absences, dinners with his "parents" on holidays, and so on. "I'll never forget the day I called him at the office and a new secretary answered the phone. She said, 'Oh, is this Mrs. Phillips? I just saw the pictures of your adorable little girl.' I thought I would die. I'd sworn I'd never fall in love with another married man, done everything I could to avoid it, and there I was again."

Devastated, Elaine went into psychotherapy. Looking at her early life, she realized that she had always competed with her older sister for her father's attention. She'd always felt second in line, second-best. "When I realized that all my great 'love' affairs with married men were really a re-enactment of my childhood feelings of always competing for the love of a man and ending up playing second fiddle to another woman, my whole life changed," she says now. "I started looking at those feelings of not being good enough to be the only woman in a man's life instead of focusing on finding 'Mr. Right.' By going to the root of the problem rather than struggling against the effects of it, I gradually began to see myself as worthy of being the wife instead of the other woman. I'm still working on it, but at least all the men I meet now are *really* single!"

By refusing to examine a pattern, we forfeit any possibility of altering our lives. If we are willing to be aware of those behavior patterns as they come up, to see them and talk about them with others, we're likely to find a gradual decline in their power to upset us. Willingness to observe a pattern objectively is the first step toward changing it.

THE STRUCTURE OF UNCONSCIOUS CONTROL

Imagine your mind as a house with a deep foundation, a ground floor, and an attic. The foundation is your unconscious mind, which contains your fundamental beliefs about who you are, what you deserve, and how the world is. The ground floor is your conscious mind, filled with the furniture of your daily life and with traffic from the outside world. The attic is your observer self, which has a broader perspective on the house and its location in the neighborhood.

Let's say that the foundation has been laid for this to be a tiny house. In terms of the mind, this might be caused by your parents' telling you (or implying) that you are not very bright, that people like you never go far in life, and that in fact the world doesn't contain enough goodies for people like you. Small conditioning, small expectations, limited foundation.

Now, suppose you come along twenty-five years later and decide those ideas are not so. Forget that limited past! You want two stories, five bedrooms, and a hot tub. You want to remodel. That's fine. Since you're also the person who issues building permits, there's no reason you shouldn't. But if you try to build the big new house on the tiny foundation, you're going to have problems. The foundation's very existence will be threatened by the remodeling on the ground floor. It may indicate that there is a conflict between the attempted remodeling and the current foundation by causing sagging walls, leaky pipes, or other small disturbances on the ground floor (nagging anxieties, uncontrollable habits, psychosomatic illnesses, and so forth).

Trying to improve your life in ways that run counter to all your previous conditioning is like trying to add a story to your house without strengthening the foundation. That inner foundation is very deep, deeper than you can get with the flashlight of your conscious mind. It's strong. If it has been laid to support a crooked house, it is much more likely to stay crooked than to straighten out on orders from your conscious mind. Yet it can be straightened out, in time. The way to begin is to empty out some of the trash that's been stored there for years; that means making room for it on the ground floor (your conscious mind) so that you can move it up and out of your system entirely and have room for something else. It's like pumping sewage out of the cellar: It may stink on the way up, but afterward the persistent reek will be gone, and you won't need to use artificial good-smell sprays (compulsive positive thinking) to make you believe that everything's fine. You will have room in the cellar to store something new (an expanded set of unconscious beliefs).

EXPOSING UNCONSCIOUS BELIEFS

Unconscious beliefs may be more noticeable in one area of our lives than another; that may explain why some people seem to have no trouble making plenty of money but can't keep a relationship together, while others have the opposite problem. One way to make life more livable is to bring unconscious beliefs into conscious awareness.

"I always thought I was very 'liberated' in my beliefs about sex," says Mike, an attorney. "I was very open about talking about it, had a lot of different partners, and really thought I was getting the most out of my sexuality. But even though I kept telling myself I had a great sex life, something seemed to be missing. I was going from partner to partner trying to find the right woman who could make me feel the sexual bliss that sex writers are always describing. A friend suggested that I write down all my beliefs about sex without censoring them. I did a whole set of sentence completions, starting with 'Sex is . . .' and 'If I truly let go sexually, . . .' and I found, to my shock, that I still had a lot of 'antiquated' beliefs about sex, like 'sex is disgusting,' 'sex is sinful,' and so on. When I got to the part about letting go, I found myself writing 'If I truly let go sexually, I would die.' No wonder I wasn't really enjoying it!"

Waking up, looking at the parts of ourselves that feel damaged and bruised, objectively looking at our own "irrational" or "unacceptable" beliefs—does that sound like a fun way to spend a Sunday afternoon? The easiest approach seems to be staying unconscious, bumping into our resistance and re-enacting childhood tragedies because we refused to experience them fully the first time around. It is also the path of least vitality.

WHAT TO DO ABOUT UNCONSCIOUS CONTROL

Knowing why we do things is important, but it is usually not enough to produce a change in our behavior. A lot of us know people who have been through years of psychotherapy and know exactly why they do the neurotic, immature things they do. But somehow they never seem to change; one might call them "knowledgeable neurotics." They're so in love with their tragic history that they'd have nothing to talk about if their lives really improved. In the end, knowing the reasons for destructive habits is useless unless that information leads us to change the way we act. In order to change our behavior, we have to *feel* those unconscious thoughts and beliefs with full force.

Deciding to regain consciousness is deciding to allow ourselves to be uncomfortable, to move past our fear of the specters stored inside, and to keep opening ourselves to new experiences and insights. The most important step in loosening the grip of unconscious control is vigilant self-observation. We have to see what we *are* doing, not what we'd like to believe we are doing. The next step is to decide to change that counterproductive behavior *without* trying to repress it out of existence.

Once you become familiar with the situations you repeatedly set up—another poor relationship with a supervisor, another betrayal by a friend, and so forth—you may begin to see that you've played a starring role in every scene. I'm not referring to unpleasantness that happens once—anything can happen once. I'm talking about the things that happen over and over again. Patterns repeat themselves as they move slowly from unconsciousness to conscious awareness. If we become a litle more objectively observant of them and of ourselves each time, they lose intensity with each repetition. Eventually, we can overcome most unconscious control by identifying patterns of behavior and "accidents" in our lives and by fully experiencing both their reality and their cost to our well-being.

There is no end to the number of things we can be unconscious about—sex, money, death, parents, siblings, deserving love, deserving money, paying taxes, anything. Every area of unconsciousness contributes to a sensation of being "out of control." Moreover, each level of unconsciousness we bring to the surface leads us only to deeper and deeper levels where more unconsciousness awaits. As one Tibetan master lamented, "It's just one insult after another."[3] For most of us, life is a continual process of peeling away layers of ignorance and delusion, only to find more of the same underneath.

This is such a cheery prospect that one might ask, "If this is true, why should we try to be more conscious at all? Why not just wallow in our unconsciousness if we'll never get through it all anyway?" This is like asking, "If I'm going to die in sixty years anyway, why should I get out of bed this morning?" Unconsciousness does diminish if we whittle away at it over time, and as we break through each level of it, we experience more vitality in every area of life.

WHAT'S GOOD ABOUT UNCONSCIOUSNESS?

For all its destructive capabilities, unconscious control does have advantages. An unconscious desire might be more life-giving than a conscious one, so its expression could do a person good. For example, Eric was very depressed after his wife, Luisa, left him. He had not known she was seeing other men and was shattered when she walked out on him one morning, never to return. In his depression, he began to think about killing himself. "I thought the only thing that would relieve my pain was death—life didn't seem worth living anymore," he says. One evening, following a long, vindictive phone conversation with his wife, Mark decided to kill himself. After pouring himself a large glass of whiskey, he methodically swallowed a large dose of pain-killers. However, he "forgot" that he had invited his brother and sister-in-law to drop by on their way home from an evening out. They discovered him passed out on the kitchen floor and called an ambulance; Eric's life was saved. He didn't "really" want to kill himself, you might say, but if you had asked him as he swallowed those pills, he would have insisted that he did. Yet some part of him did not want to die; it knew that he would recover from his heartbreak and live to love again. In this case, the triumph of the unconscious over the conscious was a triumph of life over death.

As a protective mechanism, unconsciousness also keeps

us from confronting our inner mysteries until we are ready to deal with them. "If I had realized five years ago what I know now about the destructive impulses inside me, I don't think I could have handled it," says Bill, after several years of psychotherapy. "I had such a need to see myself as a 'nice guy' that I might have gone crazy if I'd become aware that somewhere in me there are murderously angry impulses." It takes great psychological strength to confront some of the surprises inside us; unconsciousness often buffers us from devastating truth.

Another advantage of unconsciousness is that at times we become so set on the plans and ideas we've formulated rationally that we overlook crucial factors of which our unconscious mind remains aware. "I'd planned a whirl-wind 'educational' tour of the Middle East, and I thought I wanted to go on it," says Miriam, a film editor. "But as the trip approached, I began to feel exhausted all the time. I thought maybe I was anemic, so I went to my doctor. There was nothing physically wrong with me, so he asked me what else was going on in my life. I told him about the trip as one of the positive things I was planning, and he asked me if I was sure whether that was the right thing to do just then. The moment he raised the question a voice inside me started shouting, 'I don't want to go! Don't go!' I was surprised and tried to block it out, but I couldn't overlook it. The more I thought about it, I realized that in fact the trip would be stressful both physically and psychologically and that the last thing in the world I needed was more stress, especially with the jet lag that would go along with it. I hadn't real-ized how strong my inner resistance to the trip was because I was so set on going, but after thinking it over, I post-poned the trip and spent a week in the sun in Hawaii in-stead." By listening to the promptings of her inner mind, she spared herself a lot of stress (and improved her tan at the same time).

Imagine this scene: A person is striding down the street toward an open manhole. He is obviously preoccupied and determined to take the shortest route to wherever he is going. In this case, the shortest route would drop him straight into the city waterworks. Another man trots along behind him, trying to catch up in time to keep him from falling in. The first man is so intent that he doesn't hear the other's warning. Sometimes our unconscious mind is like the man frantically trying to signal someone who's walking straight into trouble, trying to warn him before it's too late. Caught up in our fixation on what we *think* is best, we may overlook the messages and warnings expressed by our gut feelings. By creating signs in the forms of mental depression, physical exhaustion, sickness, or "coincidences" that might—if we pay attention to them—make us re-examine our decisions, the unconscious mind can help us make sounder choices.

Unconsciousness is not inherently bad. It's an integral part of everyone's mental system. But if it is constricting your life or the lives of those close to you, why not commit yourself to becoming aware of the thoughts, beliefs, attitudes, and habits that are keeping you from the fulfillment you deserve?

WORKING WITH OUR UNCONSCIOUSNESS

detachment—

The best way to begin to deal with unconscious control is simply to watch it. Objective awareness of ourselves will produce more behavior change than all the resolutions in the world. After we spot our patterns, we can begin to accept their presence without necessarily acting them out. Once we stop resisting them, we may find that they play themselves out harmlessly, just as a terrifying wave dissolves into froth when it reaches the shore. Struggling against our unconscious beliefs is like arm wrestling—until one side gives in, we're putting all our energy into having nothing happen.

When our behavior mystifies us or we attract unpleasant experiences over which we apparently have no control, we are manifesting unconscious control. No matter how self-aware we become, we will slip back into old patterns from time to time or even find new, more insidious patterns that had previously been disguised by our more superficial ones. We are "forever bailing." The way out of this state of unconsciousness is to observe it with respect, love, and perhaps amusement, but without judgment or resistance. If we are truly aware of the patterns we repeat, we see how much they are costing us, and our behavior changes spontaneously. The patterns may not vanish instantly, but they will lose intensity. By watching the behavior patterns motivated by our unconsciousness, we can learn more about ourselves and become more conscious of the forces that drive us. Uncomfortable as it sometimes is, it pays to stay conscious, for the situations we create unconsciously are rarely the stuff of sweet dreams.

[handwritten margin notes:]

when we are unconscious we are repressed

this is difficult though to do, cultivating detachment requires a sort of easy/being awareness —

Detachment is not avoidance it is the simple ability to watch yourself being yourself —

when it requires too much effort you're doing it wrong —

7 CONTROLLING YOUR LIFE: A MATTER OF PRACTICE

They can because they think they can.
—Virgil

Those who think they can and those who think
they can't are both right.
—Henry Ford

Jerry Buss has about as much control over his life as a person could want. He owns the Los Angeles Forum, the L.A. Lakers, the L.A. Kings, the L.A. Lazers, and millions of dollars' worth of real estate, including his home, Pickfair, the former estate of Mary Pickford and Douglas Fairbanks, Jr. He was born to an impoverished family in a Wyoming mining town, worked his way through school (earning a Ph.D. in chemistry from the University of Southern California), and eventually went into the real estate business on one thousand dollars of borrowed money and a lot of hard work. "It's simple to become a millionaire," he says, "but it's not easy. Get a part-time job on Saturday and do it for ten years. Then take that money and invest it at 12 percent and wait ten more years, and you're a millionaire. Most people don't want to give up their free time for ten years. I've been working Saturdays since I was sixteen."

During our conversation in the living room of Pickfair, Buss said to me, "My early introduction to discipline was in education. It's impossible to go through a doctorate program in science without being very disciplined. The habits I established at that time I continued afterward. Certain small things. For instance, if I ever start a book and I find after three pages I don't like it, I still read it all the way through as an exercise in discipline. I often choose books that are very boring and dry simply because I want that discipline. In other words, I consciously put myself through discipline exercises. That's also true in my work schedule, even though I control the number of hours per week that I have to work. For instance, if I were up very late one night it would be very easy for me to sleep in the next day and cancel my appointments. I don't do that. I find that if I force myself to keep my appointments, that gives me discipline in other areas of life: I just won't stay out late on several consecutive nights. So I think my professional life is one of very definite structure.

"My social life I don't think I lead that way because I'm not so sure I want control or discipline there. I would rather live the way everyone else does." He has more control where he wants it and less control where he does not want it; this ability to choose is a sign of true control.

HOW MUCH CONTROL DO WE HAVE?

What does it mean to control our lives? In its simplest form, controlling our lives means being able to create the results we want. We want a pilot's license and we get it;

we want to be in a satisfying intimate relationship and we are; we want financial security and we have it.

Despite our possibilities for gaining control, just think of all the things we *cannot* directly control: the weather; our height; our natural talents; the emotional, intellectual, and spiritual lessons we absorbed before we learned to speak; who our parents and siblings are; whether our family has money or privilege; our primary education; the current political climate, both here and abroad; the stability of the dollar (unless you're the chairman of the Federal Reserve); and much, much more. Even our thoughts and feelings seem to come and go with a rhythm all their own. It is almost staggering to consider the extent of our powerlessness. Which may be why, when it comes to claiming to control our lives, we often protest too much.

Once we have grasped the depth to which control is a fond illusion, we can begin to exercise whatever control is possible. "Fatalist!" you might say. "Why write about controlling life if you don't believe it's possible?" I didn't say that we have *no* control; on the contrary, I do think we have a tremendous capacity for controlling both our internal state and what happens to us. It's just that we will never be able to harness that capacity until we accept its limits.

For example, we may want to fly. The first step in mastering flight is accepting that we will need some kind of machine to help us and that we will have to adapt ourselves to the laws of gravity and aerodynamics before we can succeed. Having identified our initial limitations, we begin to see how we can apply our mental and mechanical talents to help us get from New York to Los Angeles in six hours. Saying "I think I can, I think I can" and jumping out the window does not cut it. Or, as Harvey Harrison says, "Control is knowing what you can move. You can move that rock, but you can't move that mountain."

Understanding inherent constraints also includes accepting that we may not get what we want. If we refuse to accept the possibility that our plans might not work out, we deprive ourselves of the perspective that ultimately makes control possible. Sören Kierkegaard is one of many philosophers who examined the question of how much control we truly have and of how the *desire* for control actually relates to *having* control. He wrote, "If, for example, in the face of every difficulty, a young girl remains convinced that her desire will be fulfilled, . . . one can learn much from her, but there is one thing that cannot be learned from her—how to make movements [into the profound reaches of faith]—for her assurance does not dare . . . to look the impossibility in the eye."[1]

Another prerequisite for gaining control over ourselves and our circumstances is having a general idea of how much we are willing to spend—in time, energy, and money—to get that control. Some successes are not worth their cost. If we have an idea in advance of how much a particular result is worth to us, we'll know when to cut our losses and let go.

Finally, we must understand that all we are really able to control is our own mind and the way we respond to the limitations and obstacles our environment presents. This self-mastery enables us to control or work around innumerable constraints. "This guy was one of the ugliest people I've ever met, but he had women falling all over him!" says Roger of one of his friends. "He had a big nose and sort of Cro-Magnon forehead, but he was really charming. It was as though he didn't *know* how funny looking he was. He just acted like he was the handsomest man on earth; and there was something about his self-confidence that actually made people forget the way he looked."

We can envision two types of control: (1) factual control and (2) control over results. Factual control is control over the objective factors of a situation. For example, in a negotiation, one party comes to the table with more money or knowing that the other party wants or needs the deal more than he does. That puts him substantively in control. As Harvey Harrison explains, "There are objective factors, and the goal in effective negotiating is to see them very clearly." Understanding and working with the objective facts leads to more actual control, in the form of control over results. For example, when a consulting firm tries to sell a package of seminars to a large corporation, the corporation has objective control in the sense that if it doesn't buy the idea, the seminars won't be given. However, the consultants can still end up with control over results (that is, having the seminars offered at the corporation) if their ideas are valuable and they negotiate well. Control over results is what most of us think of when we think of "having control." What we do not always realize is that accepting the realities of factual control precedes control over results.

TAKING CHARGE OF OUR CAPACITY FOR CONTROL

A television documentary broadcast by KCET, Los Angeles, in 1982 reported the following story: A small village in India had suffered for centuries from the ravages of seasonal malnutrition. The villagers lived on extremely rocky land that could be cultivated only during the brief rainy season. They grew what they could when the rain came and nearly starved for the rest of the year, often complaining that if not for all the rocks, they would have more food. One day an enterprising fellow from a neighboring village suggested they gather together all the rocks and make a dam. This would enable them to trap rainwater during the wet season and use it to cultivate crops for the rest of the year. In the course of moving the rocks, they also cleared more tillable plots. Within a few years this village, which had been the poorest in its province, had the highest standard of living for miles around. What happened was that the villagers took possession of their natural ability to control. They stopped feeling victimized by their environment and turned a curse into a blessing.

All of us now have "rocks" in our lives that we "know" are blocking us from cultivating abundance. Simply by shifting to an attitude of "I have control," we begin to see options that would otherwise have been invisible. When this attitude is based on a realistic assessment of ourselves and our situation, it will not be a pretense of "having it all under control." Rather, it will give us the confidence to act.

BASICS OF CONSCIOUS CONTROL

Essentially, conscious control involves knowing what one wants, focusing on it, and then doing what's necessary to make it happen. "Positive thinkers" have been extolling the powers of the mind for a long time. While differing on certain points, all of them share the idea that the mind has a direct impact on the circumstances of life. The clearer our mental focus, the clearer our results. The connection between thought and manifestation is often plain: I think of raising my arm or turning on a light, and I do it. Since most of our actions are preceded by a thought or mental impulse, the connection between thought and physical reality seems like nothing to get excited about. But it *is*, because our thoughts also have a profound effect on what happens *to* us and *around* us. The connection occurs at more subtle and potent levels than we often suppose.

All techniques for conscious control involve *affirming*
that the thing desired already exists and *visualizing* the
current existence of the thing desired. The difference between affirmation and visualization is that an affirmation
is a verbal statement, while a visualization is a mental picture. For example, if a person wants to lose twenty pounds,
he would repeat a statement like "I am slender now" or "I
deserve to be twenty pounds thinner," either saying it
aloud or writing it down several times daily. At the same
time, he might visualize his body as it would look sans fat,
imagining that he's svelte already. This process begins to
jar the unconscious mind out of its accustomed patterns,
which, judging by the results currently being produced,
probably include affirmations like "I am a fat slob" or
"Everything I eat turns to flab" and the self-image of a fat
person. "I lost twenty-five pounds through visualization,"
says Brian, a stockbroker. "I found that when I had a clear
mental image of myself being thin, I didn't want to eat the
foods that made me fat."

In using positive affirmation and visualization as tools
for conscious creation, remember to allow for resistance.
There may be parts of us (those slippery unconscious beliefs) that don't want us to have, or don't believe we deserve to have, that wonderful marriage, high-paying job,
and home in the suburbs. If we let them babble out all
their reasons why we should *not* have what we want, they
gradually disappear. Like all of us, our unconscious mind
just wants to be listened to and loved—we don't have to
agree with everything it says. There's a natural tendency
to dislike and repress those parts of ourselves that oppose
our fabulous plans. If we can muster the self-control and
compassion to face those parts, understand their concerns,
and keep on affirming, those ogres of unconscious control
melt into nothing. Confronting the parts of ourselves that

don't want us to have conscious control is basic to *gaining* conscious control.

We also have to accept that although we'd like to think we know what's best for us right now, we might not. "I wanted that job (as credit manager of a big department store) so much—I was sure that if I could get it, my whole career would be set," says Rich. "When I got the call saying they couldn't use me, I was devastated. But two weeks later another opportunity came up and I was hired immediately. In looking back, I realize that the first job would have stuck me more in the technical end of the business, while the one I have now will enable me to branch into marketing and eventually into management. Now I'm *glad* they didn't hire me." As G. Tom Collins, real-estate broker and builder, says, "As time goes by, you come to see that things you thought were ideal would actually have been the worst mistakes you could have made. Sometimes you don't get what you want and you find out later that you are much better off." Trying hard to control our lives but assuming that if we don't get what we want, it's all for the best, takes the edge off disappointment. It broadens the tunnel vision which often comes from feeling that getting what we want is the only acceptable result.

Most of us know what we want, or what we think we want, but only the wisest of us really know (and even then only on good days) what we need. This is why many experienced "positive thinkers" recommend that we affirm for the best and most appropriate (job, relationship, resolution to a problem, and so forth) to everyone's benefit. This avoids the downside of affirmation, which is getting what you want in a way that injures you or another.

The next element in developing conscious control is (we had to get to this eventually) *work*. All the previous steps simply dispose us toward choosing the most fruitful avenues of work and set the stage for us to be open to opportunities as they come. All the energy spent on them is lost if we do not run with the ball once we have it. Although hard work in the absence of a winning attitude may not produce great results, positive thinking without work will leave you dreaming your life away. In discussing with me the impact that having control has on a person's success, Barbara Boyle, senior vice president of production at Orion Pictures, explained, "People who succeed learn more, pay their dues, and simply work harder than those who don't. For a person who really wants to succeed, there are no hours in the day; there is no 'It's six o'clock, my day is over.' When there are strictures on what you are willing to give of yourself, there are strictures on what you can achieve." We manifest our control over our lives through work.

Positive affirmation, visualization, and work, can help you produce astounding changes in your life, so long as you realize that you may never be fully in control. There are unconscious forces, cultural forces, perhaps even global forces, that influence your life. If you can permit yourself the discomfort of not knowing exactly what to do, of acknowledging distasteful attitudes that have long been plunged below the surface of your decidedly cheery conscious mind, and to accept the limitations inherent in your situation, your affirmations will work powerfully.

Truly controlling our lives means acknowledging limits, committing ourselves to set aside the limitations we've unconsciously created for ourselves, and going ahead anyway. When we do this, our conscious control will be effortless, characterized by clear intention and a sense of being carried forward by the natural stream of events.

8 CONTROLLING OTHERS: THE IMPOSSIBLE DREAM

"Kindly let me help you or you will drown,"
said the monkey putting the fish safely up in a
tree.
—Alan Watts[1]

There is nothing inherently bad about wanting to control other people; after all, it's so much more fun than controlling ourselves.

Most of us have a powerful urge to control. At one time or another we have probably felt the desire for someone else to believe like us or act like us or be the person we wish he was. That's fine; but if we let that desire for control get out of control, we end up manipulating, dominating, and generating resentment in those around us. Any parent who has tried to make a teenage child dress as the parent thinks appropriate knows what forceful resistance his or her bid for control elicits. In parent-child relationships, the parent feels justified in trying to exercise control. In other relationships, the dynamics are not so clear. Sometimes our urge to control someone else takes the guise of good intentions: "It's really in your best interest to do what *I* think you should do." Sometimes we don't even know when we're trying to control; we confuse the desire to advise another person with the need to have him do things our way because we want to be right or because we *like* things done our way.

When we are caught up in the urge to control others, it often looks as though trying to control them is our only alternative. We have the uneasy feeling that something awful will happen if we don't keep things and people under control. Where does this urge to control others come from?

It springs primarily from conflicts about control that we have not resolved in ourselves, fear of losing our personal identity, and a drive to control our environment. When we have not dealt with our inner need to control, we tend to project that need outward and try to control others. As Malcolm Forbes said to me, "It's a real sign of personal insecurity when someone is very turf-conscious. If you're secure in where you're at, you don't have to slam down." It may be tempting to try to control others because it seems as though it would be fun to live in a world where we always had our way. But though there may be financial or business benefits to slamming on the control, overindulgence in it leads to long-term personal loss—and sometimes to financial loss as well.

In the short term, it may seem possible to control another person's behavior and thoughts, but ultimately it is impossible. The impossibility of long-term control does not, of course, stop us from trying. A wife who threatens to kill herself if her husband leaves her may get him to stay for a while, but his resentment at being manipulated may ultimately make her wish he'd left in the first place. The employer who badgers and threatens his employees may feel in control for a while—but then find himself actively or covertly sabotaged by resentful employees. Using manipulation and guilt to control others makes it hard for them to keep on liking or supporting us.

Another reason we might try to influence another person's behavior is that we really do see something potentially harmful that he may have overlooked about his situation. You may try to convince a friend to give up a "harmless" daily drug or alcohol habit. A parent or teacher may try to dissuade a teenager from dropping out of school. Trying to influence or convince another person is not the same as trying to control him. The main difference is that the person who is trying to *control* another has little respect for the judgment and autonomy of the one he is trying to control, while someone who tries to *influence* knows that the other person can think for himself, and respects his ability to make his own decision.

THE URGE OF A THOUSAND FORMS

The urge to control others manifests itself in many ways, some more obvious than others. Crying, shouting, nagging, being chronically late, withholding affection, blackmail, threatening violence, threatening abandonment, authoritarianism, bullying, harassment, badgering, and just plain giving orders are among the infinite ways that people have invented to try to push others around. (Controlling others through brute force is quite different from the other forms; here we are focusing on psychological and emotional control.) Ken, the owner of an international insurance and investment corporation, was surprised one morning to receive a letter from one of his major clients that read: "I have donated two thousand dollars to my favorite charity in your name for a fund-raising dinner next month. Please reimburse me at your earliest convenience." Says Ken, "He figured that because he sends me so much business every year, I wouldn't mind—or at least that I'd have to pay it. And I did pay. But I still resent him for it." The president of a large real estate firm keeps his staff "under control" by creating an air of mystery and uncertainty about company policies. No one ever knows for sure if they will have a job the next week, so they stay alert to any hints the boss gives out. "Sure, he keeps people under control," says one of his top-producing salesmen, "but the quality people won't stand for it. I'm quitting." No one can claim that trying to control other people does not work at some level. But let's look at what it really means for us to "succeed" at controlling another person. Ken's client got the two thousand dollars, but he lost a business associate's goodwill, and that goodwill might have been far more valuable than two thousand dollars over the long haul. The real-estate big shot gained a feeling of power and importance, but he lost the base of his productivity: a competent, self-respecting sales staff. When we try to manipulate and control others, we might win at one level, but we invariably lose at several others.

"I had a friend who was *always* late," says Mary Anne, a former flight attendant. "No matter what time we were supposed to meet, she'd waltz in twenty to thirty minutes later. After a while I resented it because I realized that it was her way of trying to control me—she made me wait until it was convenient for *her* to arrive. It really bothered me, but I never had the nerve to confront her. Finally I just stopped seeing her." This is the irony of most manipulative ploys: They may help us keep other people under control temporarily, but in the end they make us lose them completely.

IS IT POSSIBLE TO CONTROL
ANOTHER PERSON?

Generations of sales trainers, politicians, and just plain folks have studied ways to get people to do what they want; the techniques have included false friendliness, expensive gifts, empty promises, and tears. Diverse as the techniques are, they have in common the manipulator's desire to control the behavior or thought (or both) of another person. Certainly products have been sold, relationships prolonged, and various desires satisfied in these ways. It *looks* as though people have been controlled. But look again.

"We've been going on this way for three years," sighs Louise. "Every time the relationship gets too painful I take myself away. I leave and don't speak to my boyfriend or call him for several months. Then when the pain of being separated from him gets too intense, I call him and we start all over again. I'm beginning to see that this 'take-away' game is a way for me to stay in control in the relationship; I can always hold it over him that if he pushes me too far, he'll lose me." Of course, the only thing Louise controls by this maneuver is how much *pain*—not how much pleasure—she experiences. In the end, her lover, Vic, felt so manipulated by her repetitive pattern of withholding herself that he wouldn't take her back. Her short-term gain turned into a long-term loss.

In India they are said to catch monkeys by setting out a small box with a tasty nut in it. There is an opening in the box that is large enough for the monkey to reach in his outstretched hand, but too small for him to withdraw the hand once he's clutched the nut. When the monkey has grabbed the prize, he must either let go of it and regain his freedom or keep hold of it and stay trapped. Unenlightened little creatures that they are, most monkeys hold onto the nut, making it easy for hunters to pick them up: box,

nut, and all. People have been known to get caught in the
same kind of trap. One might say that the person who puts
the goody in the box controls the person who grabbed it,
but is that really so? If we were willing to let go of the
goodies, we could scamper back into the forest unharmed—
and uncontrolled.

You must eventually ask, "Is it possible for one person
to control another at all?" and the answer, upon reflection,
is a resounding *no*. You can coerce, seduce, cajole, threaten,
and tempt. You can even gain a semblance of control for
a limited time, but you cannot control in the sense of
actually *making* another person do something: You cannot
control other people. Unless you have them physically in
your custody, they are free to walk. You might feel that
you *are* controlling another or that *you* are being controlled, but look carefully: It is not true. If the person
being "controlled" allows himself to be pressed into acting
contrary to his own best interest, he must take responsibility for that himself.

WHAT WE LOSE WHEN WE TRY
TO CONTROL OTHERS

Stan, a highly respected comedy writer and producer, tells
a story about an urge to control that backfired. A world-
famous screenwriter-producer was suffering from writer's
block. His agent suggested that he might overcome it by
collaborating with Stan. "For the first six weeks we were
together, I said maybe three words," Stan remarked. "He
kept saying, 'Let's get all the rules and agreements straight
before we start working. First of all, I want you to know
that even though we're splitting the money on this, I'm
the boss, so if there's any doubt about a line, it's going my
way.' It went on like this week after week. Finally I said,

'Look, I have one rule: I accept all your rules, but we start writing on Monday morning.' He said, 'Okay, but I just wanted to mention that I don't like to take more than an hour for lunch, I don't like personal phone calls, and. . . .' It was impossible to work with the guy. I walked off the project, the movie never got made, and he hasn't written anything in the seven years since."

When we have the fleeting pleasure of thinking we have controlled someone, we are not actually controlling, so much as provoking, him to make a choice. The person may allow himself to be "controlled" by us in an effort to please us, or alleviate his own guilt, or even for more concrete reasons—he may value his expense account or trust fund or social equilibrium more than his desire not to do what we ask. He is actually choosing one result over another— usually a gain over a loss or a smaller loss over a greater one. One description of this type of choice is "co-opting," which essentially means trapping a person in his own greed or fear of loss, making him an offer he cannot refuse.

John, a multimillionaire businessman, keeps his children under tight control by regulating their supply of money. "I'd like to leave Chicago and move to New York," says his thirty-year-old daughter Cathy, "but it would make Daddy very angry." We could sneer at her for allowing herself to be co-opted, but her father, who seems to have all the control, is also losing. They say that the man who pays the piper calls the tune, but in personal relationships, what's the pleasure in calling the tune? Where is the love? The mutual respect? The joy of equal exchange?

When a person tries to control another through expensive gifts or financial support, he cheats himself of satisfaction. All of us want to be loved for ourselves, not for our money or influence. If we insist on stuffing that money and influence into the pockets and lives of our loved ones, we end up with the very results we desire least:

feeling insecure and uncertain about whether and why we are loved. For example, the mother who feigns illness at every opportunity in order to keep her children close by may feel some satisfaction that they are proving their love (or at least their sense of obligation) by showing up when she complains. But since she knows (at some level) that she is manipulating them, she never knows what their true response would be. And her children are denied the spontaneous expression of their love for their mother because she weighs them down with feelings of guilt and obligation before they can say "I love you" for themselves.

Elizabeth Forsythe Hailey's best-selling novel *A Woman of Independent Means* tells the story of Bess Steed, an intrepid—and rather controlling—lady of the early twentieth century. Late in life she comes to realize that her attempts to control those she loved, especially her children, had backfired. She expresses this in a letter to her best friend: "I am determined not to repeat with my grandchildren the mistake I made with my children—using every means of coercion at my command, emotional as well as financial, to keep them close to me. Ever since Andrew [her son] came home from the war, I have had both children at my beck and call. I try to take comfort in the duty visits they pay once a week, but in my heart I am bereft. Polite strangers have taken the place of the two precious allies I sought to keep at my side forever. No mother was ever more terrified of being abandoned in her old age than I— and no mother ever did more to make it happen by doing so much to prevent it."[2]

If anything, indulging in the urge to control others causes us to completely lose control of someone who was once within our influence. We can always try to influence people, but the need to know everything they are doing or to keep them from committing some imagined betrayal

is an endless, hopeless drain on our energy. All our con-
niving for control is an exercise in futility. Why, then, do
we indulge in it?

WHAT MAKES US WANT TO CONTROL OTHER PEOPLE?

What are we really experiencing when we feel the desire to
control another person? Is it really a clear-cut wish to
dominate, or are there shards of fear and insecurity prick-
ing us from the inside, making us focus on other people's
faults instead of our own? A vague—or distinct—desire to
control another is often produced by our inner fear of losing control or of losing our sense of personal identity or
value if those around us don't agree with our opinions. It
may also be a way to keep from looking at areas of our own
personality with which we are not comfortable.

Through a mental trick called projection, we may begin to think, "It's not *me* that needs to control my eating,
it's *you*" or "It's not me that needs to quit gossiping, it's
you" and proceed to fix the other person without acknowledging that the problem is in us, not in them. Even if the
other person *does* need to control his eating or his logor-
rhea, why should it bother us so much that he doesn't? In
general, if there's a characteristic or behavior that you find
yourself constantly trying to control in other people, consider whether it is something you have not confronted or
resolved in yourself. As long as you have not controlled
that aspect of yourself, it is likely to be a source of supreme
annoyance to you when other people do it.

Even if your habitual behavior is just the opposite of
what you are trying to control in others, you may still be
fixated on it. For example, if you are always on time and

you are continually trying to train your tardy friends to be the same, you are still obsessed about time. If you never allow yourself even a bit of dessert and it drive you wild when your chubby friend digs in at the ice-cream parlor, notice that you haven't really controlled your desire for sweets—if you had, watching another person eat them would not trigger such a strong response. Whether you are on one side of a compulsion or another (always prompt or always late; anorexic or binging out), you are still trapped by *having* to do or *having* not to do. If you avoid confronting this issue internally, you may feel an irresistible desire to control other people's behavior rather than your own.

The fear of personal dissolution is also at the heart of many attempts to control others: If we base our sense of identity on a continually shifting base of feelings and thoughts—and ignore the constant presence of our observer self—we cannot help but feel insecure. When confronted by someone whose ideas and feelings are different from ours, we may feel threatened. Rather than allow ourselves to experience our own insecurity, we are likely to respond to this "threat" by attempting to control the other person. Short-haired men may want to snip the locks of longhairs; people who sip their tea with their pinky sticking out may want to train other tea buffs to do the same. The presence of someone who does things differently tells the fearful mind that its way is not the only way—and that its way may not be the best way. Rather than accept this, it prefers to stamp difference out.

If we think that the source of control and order is *outside* rather than *inside* us, then the attitudes and actions of other people take on inordinate importance. Their refusal to lend agreement to our opinions will not be experienced as legitimate and natural, but as evidence that we ourselves may be doing something wrong. There will always be differences between people, but they are outweighed by the humanity we have in common. "If people are not sure of who and what they are, then when somebody different comes along they are not able to tolerate it because in the presence of someone different, they do not feel validated. Sameness validates an insecure mind," says Judith Orloff, a Los Angeles psychiatrist.

The urge to control others has far more to do with something we are uncomfortable with in ourselves than with anything about the other person. It is likely to relate either to an unresolved conflict within ourselves or to a painful attachment to some false personal identification. Rather than acting out our urge to control others, it might be more useful if we looked to see what fears or conflicts that urge is masking. The urge to control may evaporate when we allow those fears or conflicts to come to conscious awareness. Once the urge to control others has been neutralized, we can channel our capacity to control into relationships that promote harmony and respect rather than resentment.

RECHANNELING THE URGE TO CONTROL

As long as we have the urge to control others, we might as well learn to deal with it productively. But first we have to *know* when we are actually experiencing it. Who among us wants to consider himself a manipulative or controlling bastard? Instead of admitting our impulses—which would let us choose consciously whether or not to act them out— we are tempted to claim innocently, "I'm not trying to *control* him—I just want him to do what's best." As long as we are pretending that we don't really want control, we simply stay covert about our controlling plans. If, however, we stop in midmanipulation and shift into the observer mode, we can deal with our urge constructively, without acting out. Here are some ways to rechannel the urge to control:

• *Observe with increasing clarity how, where, and why you attempt to control others.* "I never really thought of myself as a controlling person until I realized that I refused to get closely involved with anyone who was my intellectual equal," says Lee, a financial planner. "It was easy to 'hang loose' when I always knew that I was smarter and more powerful. Finally I started to notice that every time one of my peers wanted to get close to me, I tried to clamp down and regulate the relationship. It was a real eye-opener." Once we know what situations and character traits in others stimulate our need to control, we can detach ourselves from our automatic reactions and cultivate the ability to choose our response.

• *Notice whether your controlling attempts get you the results you really want.* "I think my relationship with my wife works so well because I spent so much time in previous relationships trying to be in control and I realized that it just didn't pay," says Peter, a management consultant. "I got to have my way most of the time, but I lost the love and spontaneity that I had initially entered the relationship to get." It's easy to keep repeating a deeply ingrained behavior pattern without checking to see if it is generating the results we think it is. We may *believe* that trying to control others is really a good way to gain control and that the kind of control we gain from manipulation is really what we want out of our relationships. A candid look at our actual relationships is often enough to disabuse us of this idea.

• *Note what your controlling attempts cost you in terms of health, well-being, and love.* "If people were really in touch with the *costs* of their automatic behavior patterns, they would stop them instantly," says Karen Harvey, time-management consultant. We've looked at a few of the costs of controlling—not knowing if we are loved for who we are, feeling loved for our influence instead of ourselves, provoking resentment and distrust in the people whose love and support we need most, and so forth. Extreme as these costs may be, they are not always obvious. They may manifest themselves in apparently unrelated areas of our lives—for example, in our physical health and emotional well-being. The hypercontrolling executive whose personal life is a soap opera and whose physical health is wrecked by compulsive drug use and stress is almost a cliché of modern culture. The costs are different for each of us, but they are there. What have your attempts to control others cost you?

• *Listen without preconception or judgment to others' points of view.* Sometimes other people are right. If we are more interested in retaining dominance than in solving problems, this fact may elude us. By letting the other person present his case fully without jumping in to interrupt or correct, we discipline ourselves in the art of understanding what is really happening and what others are really trying to say before we try to take control.

• *Fix ourselves when we feel the urge to fix someone else.* "My husband's fastidiousness used to annoy me more than anything else about him," says Susan, a retail-sales manager in Dallas. "I nagged him about it for years until it dawned on me that in my own way I was actually more nitpicky than he was. So actually I'd been talking to myself instead of him." The habit you hate may be your own. Eliminating our own irksome habits may "magically" eliminate them in those around us.

The potential benefits of rechanneling the urge to control are huge. When we're not busy dominating, manipulating, and fixing other people, we are better able to see them for who they are. When they in turn feel that we love and accept them as they are right now, they will be more inclined to change the parts of themselves that really are inefficient and annoying. When we let go of the need to have people do and be what we want, they are actually more likely to change. Since it is ultimately impossible to try to control another person and still maintain a feeling of fluidity and joy in a relationship, letting go of our need to control frees us to use our energy in constructive and satisfying ways.

AN URGE IS JUST AN URGE

The urge to control other people may arise from the requirements of our job, or it may come from unresolved conflicts deep in our own psyche. Whether we are paid to control other people or whether we do it on our own time, the fact remains that when we try to control with a repressive, distrustful, and disrespectful attitude, we ultimately sabotage ourselves. If we push people too far on the job, they will quit, and if we push them too far in personal relationships, they will leave. No matter how much control we think we have over another person—even when that person *believes* that we are controlling him—he ultimately controls himself. Once we realize this, the urgency is likely to go out of our urge to control. Whenever we feel like making others do, say, or feel what we want them to, we have the option to pause, take a deep breath, and see what's really going on. If our desire is based in reality, as when a shop manager wants to make an employee stop roughhousing near moving equipment, then it is appropriate to exert control—but with an attitude of firmness and respect, not manipulation. (Frequently, people are more in need of information than control; when a situation is fully explained to them, they are likely to control themselves.) By channeling our urge to control into clear communication and respect, we reach that subtle dividing line where control becomes possible through letting go.

9 SURRENDER: WHAT'S GOOD ABOUT IT?

A father sees a son nearing manhood.
What shall he tell that son?
"Life is hard; be steel; be a rock."
And this might stand him for the storms
and serve him for humdrum and monotony
and guide him amid sudden betrayals
and tighten him for slack moments.
"Life is a soft loam; be gentle; go easy."
Brutes have been gentled where lashes failed.
The growth of a frail flower in a path up
has sometimes shattered and split a rock.
                          —Carl Sandburg[1]

Now, if you breathe in and hold it, you lose your
breath; but if you breathe out it comes back to
you. So the point is: if you want life, do not cling
to it, let it go.

                          —Alan Watts[2]

Whatever you surrender to will be yours.
                          —Yogi Bhajan

In the television movie *The Day After*, a portrayal of life after a full-scale nuclear war, there is an ironic moment when the survivors hear the first postwar radio broadcast by the President of the United States. They are huddling over candlelight as they eat the last remnants of their food, watching sores fester all over their bodies as radiation sickness carries them irrevocably toward death. Every major city in the developed world has been wiped out; thousands of years of civilization have been destroyed in one day. These survivors know that their death may mark not only the end of their own lives but also of humanity. The President has these words of comfort to offer: "The damage was severe, but do not be ashamed. . . . There has been no surrender."

"I remember the first time I saw the word 'surrender' used as though it was something good," says Katherine, now the owner of a management-consulting firm. "I was browsing through a bookstore and found a record album, put out by a popular 'spiritual teacher,' titled *Love, Serve, Surrender*. My first reactions were anger and disgust. 'Service' was bad enough (were they going to pay for it?), but 'surrender'! Why would anyone want to surrender? Surrender meant humiliation, loss, defeat. The more I thought about it, the angrier I got. How dared these people encourage the public to surrender? People should fight for their due. . . . I kept fuming until I had to stop and ask myself, 'What are you so upset about? Just don't buy the album!' It wasn't until years later, after seeing many times how much energy was released through letting go—yes, *surrendering* to some forces and situations—that I understood what they meant," she says.

THE MANY MEANINGS OF
SURRENDER

Most of us think of surrender in negative terms, equating it with loss and defeat. At a dinner party, I mentioned to the young trial attorney next to me that I was writing a book describing some possible advantages of surrender. He recoiled as though I'd slapped him. "Surrender! Why would anyone want to surrender?" In military, political, and commercial pursuits, surrender is bad news. However, religious, poetic, and psychological works praise it as one of the highest goals to which a person can aspire. John Beevers writes in his introduction to Jean-Pierre de Caussade's spiritual classic *Abandonment to Divine Providence*, "Caussade was . . . obsessed by one thought: the necessity of loving God and surrendering ourselves to Him completely."[3] Hindu sage Swami Ramdas writes, "The inner voice speaks in the devotee when he has surrendered up his body, mind and soul into the keeping of the Divine who dwells within him."[4] Another Indian, Sri Ramana Maharshi, writes, "It is enough that one surrenders oneself."[5] They all seem to think surrender is a good idea.

Mystics, prophets, and poets all aspire to surrender; politicians and generals abhor it. How can this word cover such a broad range of meaning that some people would die *to* do it and others would rather die *than* do it? Perhaps it has something to do with whether our surrender has an object, and, if it does, what that object is. Surrender to God or love is far more palatable than, say, surrender to a foreign army.

On a personal level, surrender can mean going *into* situations, not away from them—not surrender *to* or *for* or *by*, but simply "surrender," an unconditional yes that propels us into new life. Particularly when the controller within us would have us hang on, surrender appears to us as it would to a military commander: a loss. But it may be wiser at times to let go.

Surrender *to* implies that the one who is surrendering has to give something up. When we are unwilling to give up, we resist. Whether it involves a child holding on to a toy or a grown-up holding on to his land, this resistance continues until the one holding on is overpowered or finds the cost of holding on too much to bear. In this context, surrender is threatening and unpleasant, easy to equate with the worst aspects of losing control. Yet there is a difference.

When we give up self-control, we are still fighting an impulse or action; we've simply lost the battle. We might try to avoid this "loss" by fighting harder the next time around. If we count to ten one day and still lose our temper, the next time we get mad we may count to twenty. Struggle, conflict, and resistance predominate. Surrender creates a completely different sensation. Through it we find the joy of diving headlong into an experience. It lets us see what happens when we allow the forces already in place to play themselves out. Surrender generates none of the frustration involved with losing control: It is beginning afresh.

If you're a giver, surrender means being willing to receive. If you're always taking, it means being willing to give. Whatever polarity you have stuck yourself in, surrender means being willing to explore its opposite. That doesn't necessarily mean *acting out* the opposite—if you've always been kind to animals, you don't have to start kicking them —but it does mean being willing to travel internally to all parts of yourself, to accept all possibilities within yourself, and to wrench yourself from the point of view you habitually hold.

Although surrender is often seen as something forced upon us by circumstance, it is fundamentally a voluntary act. The more we practice surrender, the clearer it becomes that no one can *make* us surrender. Even in war there is no compulsory surrender. (History abounds in examples of people who have chosen to die rather than give up.) Surrender is simultaneously active and passive; it is the conscious choice to give in to the forces attempting to prevail, or to pour all one's energy in a particular direction without holding back.

DEGREES OF SURRENDER

Surrenders can be interim or absolute. In interim surrender, our ultimate aim is to maintain control; in absolute surrender, we let go of control entirely. When a business mogul gives his employees free rein as long as they comply with his overall aims and desires, he is practicing interim surrender. He realizes that letting competent people do their jobs without someone breathing down their necks is good management; his limited surrender ultimately increases his control over his employees and his corporation.

In absolute surrender we are fully able to embrace the outcome of events, whatever that outcome may be. Absolute surrender is living passionately at the edge of life. It can look like breakneck living, or it can take the opposite form —joyful acquiescence to life's quirky surprises. The hallmark of absolute surrender is wholehearted action without attachment to results (a state few of us reach). As with other aspects of control and surrender, it is the spirit behind the action rather than the form of the action itself that defines the act.

For most of us, and especially for people in business, surrender is interim surrender—it takes place under an umbrella of control. In fact, what many people might call surrender is actually indirect control. Alan Platt, senior analyst at the Rand Corporation, clarifies this when he says,

"Things are getting so complex and technology is moving so quickly that it's hard to maintain the kind of single control that previous generations could exercise. What you have to do is retain residually the sense and appearance of authority, and perhaps the ultimate authority."

What really distinguishes surrender from indirect control is our willingness to have things take whatever form they will, regardless of whether that form matches our expectations. "Whether or not we can really allow something to take place outside of our control and accept the consequences one way or another, that's what surrender is all about," says Allen Hershberg, a stockbroker at a major brokerage house. The entrepreneur who appears quite "surrendered" because he throws all his resources into an enterprise knowing full well he could lose everything is often in fact motivated by a powerful desire to control. He may risk all he has and lose it several times over, but always in an attempt to reach a goal, to corner a market. He is willing to risk everything, having understood that the path to great control is one of great—if not absolute—surrender.

All surrender requires trust. Interim surrender requires limited trust and absolute surrender requires vast trust: in the universe, in ourselves, and in other people. The more trusting we are, the easier it is to practice dynamic surrender.

THE FOCUS OF SURRENDER

There is a crucial difference between internally and externally focused surrender. Externally focused surrender is directed toward someone or something outside ourselves— an authority figure, perhaps. Internally focused surrender is letting go *of* something within ourselves *to* something within ourselves—for example, surrendering the need to belittle others to the part of ourselves that motivates us to act with consistent compassion.

Internal surrender can be complicated by the fact that we tend to be more attached to certain of our desires than to others. One person may be willing to give up all his money but refuse to let go of his pride; another may be willing to sacrifice pride and self-respect in return for money. *What* a person surrenders, and what he surrenders *to*, say a lot about what he considers important in life.

A beneficial type of dynamic inner surrender is letting go our preconceptions and established points of view. Being willing to set aside what we *think* is true facilitates us in finding out what is really true. Another type of dynamic inner surrender is surrender of the ego to the natural rhythm of life, God, the universe, or whatever one conceives of as a higher or more expanded force. Since the desires and opinions of our ego constitute much of our sense of personal identity, it may be hard to imagine giving up the ego without giving up our essential nature. But if we give it up by consciously surrendering it to something beyond us, we discover that we are in fact more than our ego. There is somebody left after the surrender: our observer, or "higher," self. Surrender to a divine or cosmic force may also bring us into closer contact with the force; these moments of union or communion are often described as mystical.

THE ABILITY TO SURRENDER:
WEAKNESS OR STRENGTH ?

"I'd never surrender voluntarily," says Jerry, a shoe-manufacturing executive from New Jersey. "I'm really a very strong person—it seems to me that the guy who gives up first is obviously weak." If life were like arm wrestling, this would be true. But it's not. Is it really a sign of strength never to give in, retreat, or surrender? Psychologists and statesmen both agree that a never-say-die attitude is more a liability than a strength.

In professional football, coaches use the phrase "reckless abandon" to describe the way their special teams should rush the opposing linemen. "All good football players should play with reckless abandon," says Mike, a former professional player. Throwing themselves into the game— surrendering to it—helps them win. In psychological terms, the ability to surrender can be seen as flexibility, a willingness to move from a fixed position into one more consonant with the necessities of a situation.

"The psychoanalytic view suggests that one must have a strong ego first in order to truly lose it," says Harry Brickman, a psychoanalyst and former director of the Los Angeles County Department of Mental Health. Those who try to surrender without first developing mental flexibility and the willingness to face the hitherto unconscious contents of the mind may disintegrate under the pressure of a powerful "self-abandonment," or inner surrender. Thus, it actually takes more strength to surrender than to control: A strong and adaptable ego is a prerequisite to dynamic surrender, and the ability to surrender is essential to mental health.

THE VALUE OF DYNAMIC SURRENDER

"I was dating a man quite a bit older than me, even though I knew I wanted to have a serious relationship with someone nearer to my own age," says Janet, a psychotherapist. "I kept thinking that as soon as I met someone younger, I'd break up with Ben. But I didn't meet anyone else. After several months, I resolved to break up with Ben completely,

even if it meant being alone for a while. Within a few weeks
a fascinating (younger) man told me he'd been attracted to
me for a while but hesitated to ask me out because he knew
I was involved. Now he and I are developing a very close
relationship." Frequently, improvements in our lives only
come after we've made room for them. By unequivocally
ending our previous condition, we create the space for a
new one and open possibilities for results beyond our
greatest dreams. Nothing can be added to a room that's
already full of furniture, nor can anything be contributed
to a life crammed with overactivity or a mind full of fixed
positions and ideas. Surrender is the prelude to creative
emptiness.

LETTING GO OF WHAT WE
DON'T NEED

Marjorie, a hairdresser, says, "I never realized how attached
I was to the feeling of being better than other people until
my best friend pointed it out to me and told me to cut it
out. 'What makes you think you're so great?' she asked, and
I had to admit that I couldn't justify my superior attitude.
I decided to get rid of that tendency but found that getting
rid of it was a lot harder than I'd thought. I really needed
to feel that I was better than everyone else, and I *wasn't!*
The biggest revelation for me was when the same friend
asked me, 'What do you need that attitude for?' and I
realized that all it did was cover up my insecurities. Somehow, after that it got easier to let go of it because I saw
that I really didn't need it."

If we have something we don't want, what is there to do
with it but let it go? Each of us has habits, relationships,
character traits, and much more that we do not want—yet

it rarely seems to occur to us that we could simply let these things go. We could let go of our prejudices and negative expectations about life, our unwillingness to love, our compulsions, and our tendency to change television channels every ten minutes, all without threatening our essential well-being. If we do not feel we can surrender without surrendering *to* some external force, we can imagine that we are surrendering these aspects to God, our "higher self," or simply to our capacity to be our best self. If we have the urge to surrender but direct it toward a life-negating object, however, we may create more problems for ourselves than we had at the start.

MISGUIDED SURRENDER: FATALISM AND FOLLY

Jamie, a bright, articulate former college student, came from a disciplined household where he was expected to produce good grades as well as follow his parents' moral principles. He did his best to please and in fact was doing quite well before he discovered "surrender." Tagging along to a meeting of followers of a "guru," he was exhorted to give up his bourgeois baggage and renounce the illusions of the world. This renunciation involved donating all his money to the guru, dropping out of school, wearing unusual clothes, and engaging in unrestrained promiscuity—in short, "letting go." After twenty-three years of struggling to do things "right," Jamie thought this sounded great.

He renounced everything, doing his best to follow his teacher's instructions to surrender fully to him and to live only in the moment. Looking back, he says, "At the time, I really believed I was fulfilling some spiritual goal of surrender. I'd participated actively for several years before I realized that doing whatever my teacher told me to, even when it was contrary to my instincts, was not necessarily true surrender. I had stopped my education and worked without pay for the organization. I couldn't sustain a committed relationship (it's hard to do when you're only following the impulses of the moment). I finally got out, and now I feel like I'm starting life all over again in my late twenties. I can't say I'm completely sorry I did it, but I do have some regrets."

There are two basic ways a person can surrender with devastating effects for himself and those around him: arbitrary surrender to a life-negating force, and excessive fatalism. The more pernicious misuse of surrender is the "surrender" that ultimately denies free choice and which leads the one who surrenders to injure himself or others. Such surrenders can be to an ideal, an individual, or a group. Foolish and misguided "surrenders" have appeared in many centuries, including our own. Nazism, Jonestown, cults—as diverse as they may be, they shared an ability to manipulate followers into "surrendering" to a so-called higher cause that eventually led to ruin. Note that in these cases it was not the *process* of surrender that was destructive. The tragic consequences of life-negating surrender ensued because the followers were unable—or unwilling—to see their behavior objectively and re-examine it in the light of reason and their intuitive sense of well-being, and because the leaders misdirected them into serving their own megalomania and destructiveness.

Fatalism, the second major abuse of surrender, is really a justification for inaction. Although the first step of surrender is surrender to circumstances in the sense of recognizing and accepting facts, once one has surrendered to the facts, one can throw oneself fully into changing them as much as possible. The fatalist overlooks this. He claims that if a process is already set in motion, there's nothing he can do, so he might as well "surrender" to it. In some cases this is true, but it takes a keen and discriminating mind to say for certain when enough effort is enough.

The person who habitually takes the position "there's nothing I can do" is not manifesting an ability to surrender; he is abdicating personal responsibility and submitting indiscriminately to circumstance. Statements like "I was born poor, my parents were poor, therefore I'll die poor" or "If it weren't for those people (institutions, or whatever) I wouldn't be in this situation" exemplify this attitude. Taking the position that every option in our lives has already been determined leads us not to dynamic surrender but to capitulating before we have participated fully in life. Rather than surrendering *to* this self-destructive attitude, we're better off surrendering the attitude *itself*. That means letting go of fatalism and surrendering to action in the world.

Surrender is not necessarily the most appropriate response to every situation. As with self-control, the key word is *choice*. If you always surrender without looking at your options or at the effects of your action (or inaction), you have not chosen to surrender: You have acted out a compulsion. Only machines react in the same way to every stimulus; that's what makes them machines.

LETTING GO FOR OUR OWN GOOD

We must distinguish between life-serving and life-negating surrender and focus on the former. As we explore our capacities for surrender, we see two directions surrender can take: surrender that destroys life (surrender to addictions, fanaticism, other obsessive behaviors) and surrender that enhances life (surrender to love, growth, whatever nurturance life can offer). We can make it a point to always surrender to some situation or state of awareness that is freer and more expanded than our current one.

It may not be easy to determine whether a particular surrender will serve or negate life. However, if we commit ourselves to honestly asking which direction our projected surrender will take us in, we may find that we instinctively know the truth. We can remember two basic parameters to help us make our choice: well-being—our own and that of others—and results. If well-being and results are diminished after the surrender, it may have been a life-negating choice. Surrender *can* mean capitulation or defeat if it is to something strong yet life-negating, such as an enemy or an addiction to dangerous substances. However, surrender to life-expanding situations, such as being loved or being a winner, gives us a renewed sense of power and vitality.

Surrender to winning can be very difficult, since it means letting go our notions that we're not good enough, that our critics are right, that we should never have gone back to school after the first day of kindergarten. Many of us are so conditioned to accept limitation and defeat that it is a tremendous challenge for us to surrender to our own good.

Take a moment and look through your inner catalogue of attitudes and beliefs. Look at the people closest to you; look at the way you spend your time. Think about the distinction between life-serving and life-negating surrender: Which of your attitudes, companions, and activities could you let go of as a practice in life-serving surrender? Given all the opportunities available to you right now through surrender, what do you most want to surrender, in the sense of releasing it from your life; and what do you most want to surrender *to*, in the sense of making more space for it? Once you know what your life-serving surrenders are, you can choose them.

EXCITING (AND UNAVOIDABLE) SURRENDER

No matter how we try to avoid it, we must eventually confront the issue of surrender. Surrender is essential to the rhythm of our daily lives. The traffic light turns red and we stop for it; we get on a plane and let the pilot fly it; market research indicates that our idea for a new product will not succeed and we modify it. Not only in countless daily details but in the very basis of our bodily function, surrender is inherent to life. Every muscular movement is based on one muscle group's "letting go" while its complement tenses up. We cannot live unless we are willing to let go of each breath to make room for a fresh one. (Taking a deep breath is actually an excellent tool for disposing us to let go.)

Everything ends in surrender, because everything begins in surrender. Surrender relieves us of the status quo. It creates space. We may fear it, but we can never escape it. Every breath, every heartbeat, every moment of brain function depends on the process of control and surrender. Contraction and expansion, stimulation and rest: We could not live if our bodies were not capable of surrendering one moment in favor of the next.

Like breathing, surrender is a continuous process. One moment you take things in, and the next you let them go. Moments of surrender may be followed by moments of self-control, which give way naturally to new surrenders. Each moment of surrender is important, even if its effect on our lives is not immediately apparent. The breath you thoughtlessly take as you park your car has less obvious impact on you than the one you take after nearly drowning. Yet each one sustains life. In the same way, each breath of surrender creates a seed of new life.

10 "I CAN'T LET GO!": FEAR OF SURRENDER

A man went for a stroll on a deserted cliff. Straying too close to the edge, he fell and ended up clinging to a scraggly bush halfway down. He looked at the abyss below him and up at the bush, which was slowly but steadily becoming dislodged under the strain of his weight. He called up toward the top of the cliff, "Can someone please help me? Is anybody up there? Anyone *at all?*"

The clouds parted, and a preternatural light shone through. The voice of God thundered down from heaven, saying, "I will help you, my son. Just let go of the branch and I will hold you up."

A long pause. Looking up again toward the top of the cliff, the man shouted, "Anybody else?!"

"I remember the first time I really confronted my fear of surrender—I had to be forced into it," recalls Michael, a screenwriter in his mid-thirties. "I was in my early twenties, and all sorts of conflicts that I'd tried to suppress through-

out my childhood—about my father's death and all the
pain surrounding it, all of it—started to bubble to the surface. I tried to keep pretending they weren't there. But the
internal pressure built up until I felt like I was about to
burst. I wanted to scream but was afraid that if I started
screaming, I might never stop; I thought I would burst into
pieces if I let all that pressure out at once. At the same time,
I knew I couldn't go on the way I was.

"Finally, I went to a Buddhist meditation center up in
the mountains to sort the whole mess out. The pressure got
to a point where I felt that even though I might burst if I
did scream, I would also burst if I *didn't*. So I had nothing
to lose.

"I picked my way across some rocks and stood alone in
the center of a clearing; I'd made up my mind to scream
until I couldn't scream anymore. I stood there half-choking,
wanting to let go, *determined* to let go, but still terrified
that I'd explode if I did. Finally, I thought about my father's
death, about everything I'd never fully felt or said throughout my life. My mouth opened up and I started to scream.
At first it sounded strange and hoarse, but then it got
stronger and louder. God bless those Buddhist monks—nobody bothered me or told me to stop.

"To my amazement, what happened was the opposite of
what I'd feared. Instead of bursting open in a destructive
way, I found that with every scream something inside me
was relieved. I stopped after ten or fifteen minutes—that
was the other surprise, that this supposedly bottomless pit
of pain could have been expressed in less than an infinity—
and I could breathe deeply again. The pressure was gone.
I went into the meditation hall and sat with the other visitors
at the center."

At some level, we are always choosing between control and
surrender. Often it is not a question of whether surrender

is the most appropriate choice, but whether we can overcome our fear of it. I know for myself that every surrender,
no matter how petty, is preceded by a hesitation, a moment
when I stand like a child at the edge of a diving board
wondering whether I'll crack my head if I jump. There's
doubt about whether to hold on a little longer or let go now.
It may only last a second, but that instant contains the fear
of dying, the fear that the world will dissolve if I don't hold
it together, the fear of being a fool, and other nameless
terrors. I let myself experience that fear and then let it go.
On the other side of it I invariably find there is indeed a
pool under the diving board.

Seeing our fear of surrender is the first step in overcoming it. Why overcome it? Because like the mythical hero
Jason, who had to tame a fearsome dragon before he could
reach the Golden Fleece, we must go past our fears if we
hope to reach the treasures of creativity and life within us.
Mastering our fear of surrender by confronting it and
surrendering anyway gives us a power and self-confidence
that is forever closed to us if we cower at the unknown
within.

TOO LATE: YOU'RE ALREADY
SURRENDERING

All of us begin by surrendering to birth and end by surrendering to death. Not only every heartbeat but every
orgasm, every moment of love is made possible by our
capacity for surrender. Do we fear these? Do we want to
stop them?

Feeling "I'm afraid of surrender" is similar in many
ways to feeling "I'm afraid of breathing." Many of us are
in fact afraid of breathing deeply and of the vitality that

unrestricted breath gives us. We show this by refusing to take, or seeming to be unable to draw in and fully expel, a series of deep breaths. Halfway in and halfway out goes the air, and every diminished breath constitutes a moment of diminished life. In the same way, we may express our fear of surrender by never quite letting go, always keeping one foot on the firm ground of control as we pretend to be exploring the open seas of surrender. As a result, we never get anywhere: never fully in control, never fully in surrender. We do not get the satisfaction of true release.

The irony of this elaborate avoidance is that surrender is at the heart of life. We are always doing it. We may surrender gracefully or kicking with resistance, but surrender we do, whether we like it—or fear it—or not.

Some people might say that it's smart to avoid surrender in a random and disorderly world such as our own. "I don't need more surrender," they may say, "I need more control." If such a person would consider the long-term costs of his relentless efforts to gain more control and remember the value of whatever brief moments of life-serving surrender he might have experienced, having more control might not seem like such a prize.

When the fear of surrender stops us from choosing life-serving surrenders, it is not helping us. This fear is rooted in the belief that we live in a disorderly and destructive universe ready to gobble us up if we ever quit fighting for control. But the most casual glance at the natural world provides countless examples of supreme and life-giving order. Over time, all natural processes arise, crest, and subside. Whether we look at geologic eras, tides, civilizations, or the emotions of an individual person, this rhythm of "arising, abiding, and ceasing to be" (as it is described in Buddhist philosophy) is incessant. It *is* remarkable that the sun rises and sets so regularly, century after century. Plants, animals, the progression of the seasons—everything around us indicates benevolent order. Within this order there is disorder, to be sure—violence between and within species, for example—but if we were to observe a tapestry of life on this planet from its inception to the present, we would see a regular pattern of birth, flowering, death, and renewal that could quell the fears of the most entropy-fearing among us. Even events that appear unnatural and disordered often turn out to fit perfectly in an orderly plan that was not apparent at the moment the "disorder" hit. As basketball star Magic Johnson said in an interview in the *Los Angeles Times* (March 7, 1984), looking back at a knee injury that kept him on the sidelines for forty-five games, "The injury was a blessing in disguise. It made me see that everything came fast and good and that it could easily be taken away just as fast. I see things differently now."

It is *possible*, despite appearances to the contrary, that things will turn out fine if—at least sometimes—we simply allow them to take their course. Physicians know that nearly 80 percent of the complaints for which patients consult them would resolve themselves whether the person saw a doctor or not. Talking to the doctor and getting "medicine" for the problem satisfies the need to *do* something rather than let the sickness run its natural, usually limited, course. In the other 20 percent of cases, the patient really does need something done right away, and the delay in getting treatment can be damaging. But the odds favor the two greatest medicines: patience and time.

Ultimately, things will arise, abide, and cease to be whether we like it or not. Our main choice is whether to go along with this process smoothly or bunch up against it in resistance and fear.

FEAR OF SURRENDER AND THE
FEAR OF DEATH

> Few participate in their life so fully that death
> is not a threat, is not the grim reaper stalking
> just beyond the dark windowpane. Most fight
> death as they fought life, struggling for a foot-
> hold, for some control over the incessant flow of
> change that exemplifies this plane of existence.
> —Stephen Levine[1]

If we are caught up in the belief that we are nothing more
than the collection of flesh, bones, thoughts, and emotions
we label "I," the notion of surrendering may reek of death.
Belief in the limited self leads us to equate surrender with
death, and many everyday uses of the term seem to back
this up. Military surrender is seen as a form of death, and
in fact it is, in the sense that it is the end of an era, the death
of a historical phase. But the death of a phase is not the
same as the death of a being. Surrender is not the end of
the world, even though the apprehension preceding it may
make us *feel* that it is.

It may be that to the extent we fear death, we will fear
surrender; however, as Stephen Levine points out, to the
extent that we fear death, we also fear life. Perhaps we can
learn something about overcoming the fear of surrender by
looking at the way the terminally ill overcome their fear of
death. Elisabeth Kübler-Ross, author of *On Death and
Dying*, points out that those who resist the acknowledgment and the experience of death suffer most as their mor-
tality closes in: "In other words, the harder they struggle
to avoid the inevitable death, the more they try to deny it,
the more difficult it will be for them to reach this final stage
of acceptance with peace and dignity."[2]

Much of what Kübler-Ross and Levine have discovered

about the fear of death can be related to our fear of surrender, since dynamic surrender *is* like death: It is an un-
equivocal passage into the unknown. Every great religious
tradition speaks of the necessity of "dying unto oneself," of
surrendering—in the service of a greater power—everything one had or thought one was. Surrender is a form of
death within life, a death through which we are reborn
over and over again—into life.

Surrender marks the end of one period and the beginning of another. It is both frightening and exciting. If we
focus on the fearful aspect, we don't find out what surprises
the universe has in store for us—or if we do find out, we'll
feel that they were foisted on us. If we focus on the exciting
aspect, then life is one long series of Cracker Jack boxes: a
surprise in every package.

It is no accident that mystics, when writing of their
transcendent spiritual experiences, describe their blissful
state as a type of death and consider the willingness to "die"
a prerequisite of mystical surrender. Muhammad said, "Die
before ye die"; a Tibetan master said, "Give up thy life, if
thou wouldst live"; a Zen master said, "Those who cling to
life die, and those who defy death, live." The great Christian
mystic St. John of the Cross used the image of death exten-
sively in his writings, not as something to be avoided, but as
something to be longed for. St. John longed for the death
of the individual self, which would lead to his communion
with God. In his poem "I Live Yet Do Not Live in Me," he
wrote:

> I live yet do not live in me,
> am waiting as my life goes by,
> and die because I do not die.[3]

Rather than fearing physical death, St. John fears the
spiritual death that results from not giving oneself up to, or

"dying" into, God. He longs for God and understands that
in total surrender we vanish utterly into the force to which
we surrender. These mystical "deaths" are followed by re-
birth into a fresh and more vibrant life.

GETTING OVER THE FEAR OF
LETTING GO

"People kept telling me I was crazy not to try to stop Allen
from seeing his secretary outside the office," says Connie.
"But I knew that if we were meant to stay together, we
would, so I didn't try to resist it; I just stayed as beautiful
and loving as I could. I've seen so many women drive their
husbands into long-term bonds with women who might
have only been passing flirtations—just from not trusting
the basic soundness of their marriage. He knew I wasn't
happy about the affair, but he also knew that I loved him
enough to stay with him until he got it out of his system.
And he did." Connie was remarkable in her self-confidence
and trust; she knew that she was uncomfortable, but was
able to deal with her fear of losing her husband without
acting out that fear in a way that drove him away.

The first step in overcoming this fear is observing and
clearly acknowledging it. If we can allow ourselves to fully
experience this fear, we see that there is in fact an end to
it, that on the other side of the fear is the placid power of
fearlessness. Our experience of the fear may take the form
of trembling and nausea, of emotional sensations, or of
mental images. Whatever form it takes, if we allow it to
come over us, it will pass much more quickly than we
anticipated. For some people, confronting the fear of surrender can be a shocking and upsetting experience. If you
have any question about whether you have the emotional

strength to experience it on your own, I recommend that
you consult a qualified mental health professional.

Another way to overcome this fear is to observe how
many things in nature and in human life actually *do* work
out. Think of all the cars on the road that *don't* have accidents; think of all the babies born with all systems go. We
often fear surrendering because we think something awful
is about to happen and we don't want to allow it. But think
back on all the times when you have interfered in relationships and situations. Of course there were times when you
saved the day, but think about the ratio: How many times
did the dreaded event happen anyway? How often did you
prevent something from happening and then find that your
victory had no value? How often was the fear and resistance
worth the time and energy spent on it? As we attune ourselves to the benevolent order of the universe and allow
ourselves to fall into alignment with it, we diminish our
need to cling to the fear of surrender.

Still another way to overcome the fear is to notice it and
let it be there, but surrender anyway. Louise, now an executive in a multistate real estate syndication firm, says, "When
they offered me the vice presidency, my first thought was,
'I'll never be able to do it; they must be making a mistake.'
I was afraid of allowing myself success. But the more I
thought about it, I realized, 'Why should I resist? Success is
coming to me and I'm telling it to find someone else.' So I
went ahead and took the job. It's only a year later and
already I feel like I've been doing it all my life."

If you want to take an even more active role in overcoming your fear of surrender, try this: Make a mental or
written list of all the subjects that stimulate your fear of
surrender. (Writing them down is preferable.) For example,
you may feel very confident about taking risks in your business life but freeze up at the prospect of an intimate relationship, or you may be quite gregarious and socially in-

volved but become rigid and distrustful when confronted with a new idea about politics or religion. In such cases, your fear of surrender relates to opening up mentally. Some people are quite open intellectually but refuse to allow themselves to experience new physical challenges, such as skiing or rock-climbing. Everybody has something.

If your fears are reality based—if, for example, you're afraid of getting involved with someone who is psychologically unbalanced, or if you're afraid to take up skydiving because you have a heart condition—then what you're experiencing is not fear of surrender: It's common sense. But if you can envision doing the thing you're afraid of and growing from it, then resolve to do it. Deliberately put yourself into a position where your fear of surrender will be triggered, and act in spite of it. Your pleasure will be twofold: in experiencing something new and in overcoming a fear that had been blocking you.

TAKING THE PLUNGE

As we begin to experience the fear of surrender as a factor in our decisions about what we allow to happen to us in life—taking a new job, starting a new relationship, having a baby, committing ourselves to a spiritual practice—we learn to distinguish between fearing surrender and blocking a truly destructive force. If a truck is bearing down on us as we cross the street, it is not fear of surrender that makes us run to the other side—it's our desire to stay alive. But if a wonderful person offers us friendship and love and we hold back, trying to decide whether or not to let this new warmth in, then we need to examine ourselves for fear of surrender.

Fear of surrender is a natural precursor to surrender itself. We tend to fear surrender partly because we are trained so thoroughly to avoid it and partly because it requires us to leap into the truly unknown. It's scary not to know. Surrender often looks like loss, and sometimes it really feels like loss, but once we go through it, we see that it's all gain.

Inner surrender begins with experiencing our terror at the prospect of letting go. It ends in perceiving the love and generosity that lie hidden behind our veils of denial. Surrender upon surrender makes us unafraid of life.

11 EASY DOES IT: SURRENDER STEP BY STEP

I died from minerality and became vegetable;
And from vegetativeness I died and became
   animal.
I died from animality and became man.
Then why fear disappearance through death?
Next time I shall die
Bringing forth wings and feathers like angels;
After that, soaring higher than angels—
What you cannot imagine,
I shall be that.
                    —Mevlana Jelalu'ddin Rumi[1]

"When Richard and I first started making love, I could hardly let him touch me," says Rene, whose first husband had beaten her frequently. "I flinched every time he reached out to me, no matter how gentle he tried to be. I can't believe he was so patient. But gradually I started to realize that he really did love me—that I could trust him. He took it very slowly, from stroking my hands and face to more intimate touching. We went through a lot of steps before we could really make love, but I think it was worth it for both of us."

Throughout our lives, each of us goes through our own
stages of surrender. Whether we are gradually coming to
terms with getting older or accepting our own frailties and
the frailties of those we love, life forces us to surrender to
the way things are. We may also gradually develop our
ability to surrender to the creative impulses that drive us
on, or to God as we perceive Him. Life is one long opportunity to surrender. And we do surrender, each of us at his
own pace. We may not always realize that what we are
learning *is* surrender; only in looking back at the tightly
wound-up people we used to be do we realize how much
we've let go.

As in any process of growth, surrender comes in steps—
some big, some small. The stages set out below are not intended to prescribe the steps you *must* go through as you
expand your capacity for surrender, but rather to describe
some of the stages that seem natural as the process unfolds.

No one expects a plant to grow from a seedling into a
tall tree overnight or a child to go from crawling to running
in a day. Yet we often expect immediate transformation in
ourselves. When we have this expectation, we cannot help
but be disappointed. We cannot become a new person overnight, and even when we have changed dramatically for the
better, we are sure to act inconsistently from time to time.
One moment we may be ecstatically open to whatever the
universe sends our way, and the next moment we may be
angrily kicking a jammed bathroom door. This is natural.
We are not machines, moving consistently from one step
to another. We are people, who may be quite open-minded
at the prospect of accepting the limitations of our car but
go a little crazy at the prospect of accepting the limitations
of our kids. Inconsistent though we may be, there is a
ratchet effect—two steps forward, one step back—which
keeps us slowly but steadily moving ahead if we allow it.

In *Who Dies?* Stephen Levine describes the discomfort

that arises unavoidably when we let go of our habitual way of viewing ourselves in favor of a new way. Even if our previous attitude had constricted our pleasure and productivity, it was ours; it felt comfortable. Levine says that holding on to that previous attitude is like carrying a heavy piece of baggage through a station as we rush to catch a plane or train, until at last we reach our seats: "As we begin to open our hand, we find it cramped around the handle of that old baggage. It is difficult, even painful, to return the hand to its natural openness, because the force of holding has so contracted it. Cramped by its holding, its return to the natural state is slow and occasionally discomforting. Because we so fear pain, we prefer to remain contracted rather than allow the release of ancient tension."[2]

LETTING GO OF WHO WE ARE FOR WHO WE COULD BECOME

> He who would be what he ought to be must stop being what he is.
> —Meister Eckhart

If we assume that the search for self-actualization (whether we perceive that to be a psychological or a spiritual state) is essential to our well-being, then passing from stage to stage of surrender seems inevitable. For us to be greater than we are now, we must give up our current limits. The image of the nautilus snail illustrates this. The nautilus is a tiny snail that, like all snails, creates a shell it carries on its back. It differs from other snails in that it creates a new, expanded compartment to live in as it grows. When the "new house" is ready, the creature pushes itself, with great effort, out of the smaller shell and into the bigger one. It then seals off the smaller compartment, so it can never go back. It keeps growing and goes to work on the next-bigger compartment. As human beings we can expand our capacities or even throw off our shell completely, learning from the nautilus snail as it patiently and steadily expands its abode. This prospect is both frightening and exciting: frightening because it means giving up the known comfort of our current "shell," exciting because of the possibilities that lie before us. It takes courage to commit ourselves to discovering who we could become. This courage and commitment carry us forward even when our fear would hold us back.

WHAT ARE THE STAGES OF SURRENDER?

The stages of surrender are like the stages of a great love affair—first there is resistance and uncertainty, but this leads gradually to surrender of the mind and body, with nothing held back. Here is an outline of the stages as they appear to me:

1—*Unconsciousness and denial*
2—*Resistance and struggle*
_____
3—*Acknowledging the fear of surrender*
4—*Confronting the fear and cleansing ourselves*
5—*Conditional surrender (taking a chance)*
6—*Going overboard*
7—*Balancing*
8—*Dynamic surrender in everyday life*

Not everyone passes through all the stages of surrender; many stay in unconsciousness and denial all their lives. That's why there is a line between steps 2 and 3. Struggle can perpetuate itself endlessly. The moment when we reflect on the *source* of our struggle is a turning point. As we do so, we may become aware of the sucking whirlpool of terror that lies below the unreflective mind. Our first glimpse of this fear can be shocking, but acknowledging it is the first step in our transformation. As long as we are barricaded behind our resistance, all we get is more of the same. At a certain point, though, when we allow ourselves to experience the fear and begin to explore its boundaries, the balance shifts. We are drawn on to explore the enormous world that lies beyond our desperate efforts to hang on. "Each step is taken with love, not forcing the edge but softly penetrating our imagined limitations and going beyond, step by step, into the freedom of nonholding," as Stephen Levine puts it.[3]

Let's look at one person's passage through the stages of surrender. Your own circumstances may be different, but you and Gene may have something in common. Our sample surrenderer is a businessman in his midforties, married to a woman named Carol. He went to decent schools and has a decent job as a vice president (one of many) at a tool-and-die-manufacturing company. He has two children—a twelve-year-old daughter and a fifteen-year-old son. Many years ago he cut himself off from his male friends. He rarely exercises but still considers himself to be "in good shape." Every evening after work, he has at least one cocktail, to help him "unwind." In the last few years, his sex drive has diminished, but he is sure that this is due to the onset of middle age—or to something that's wrong with his wife. He thinks he's a good guy, and at heart, he is. What he doesn't know is how deeply out of touch he is with the rest of life. Here is his story:

1—*Unconsciousness and denial.* This is where most, perhaps all, of us begin. When we're unconscious, we don't *know* that we're unconscious; that's why we can stay unconscious for a long, long time. Ask an unconscious person about himself and he'll say, "I'm fine"; ask everybody around him and they'll say, "This guy is asleep at the wheel."

For Gene, or anyone else who lives in unconsciousness and denial, either the subject of surrender is nonexistent or the mention of it puts him to sleep. He changes the subject. That someone is unconscious about surrender in no way diminishes its power in his life. In fact, the more he denies it, the more powerful it becomes.

When his secretary complains about an annoying habit Gene has, he listens to her but does not change his ways. Any tremors of unrest in his marriage he ignores. He suspects his son might be experimenting with drugs but dismisses his suspicions with the thought "No kid of mine would do a thing like that." His eyes are open and he is walking around, but Gene is unconscious. He is denying all indications from his mind and environment that something is awry.

2—*Resistance and struggle.* Carol asks Gene to take her to dinner at their favorite restaurant. Over coffee, she tells him that she cannot bear the emotional isolation of living with him any longer: She wants a trial separation. He does not know what she is talking about. She goes on to say that the school psychologist called her a few days before and told her their son had been caught skipping classes and smoking marijuana on the athletic field with some other boys.

Enraged, frightened, shocked, Gene sputters and fumes. "What do you mean, a trial separation? Haven't I always been a good husband? What's wrong with our relationship? We never argue! And as for that rotten son of mine, he's not too old to get a beating he'll never forget." Gene is resisting the evidence that the life he thinks he has is a rigidified dream. He is struggling against acknowledging the truth.

At this point he has a choice. He can continue to maintain that his perceptions are right and everybody else is crazy. If he does this, he will almost certainly lose his wife and children. If he is very brave, or if the emotional cost of losing his family would be too terrible to bear, he may agree to examine his role in the creation of this mess. If he chooses this course, one of the first things he will encounter within himself is his fear of surrender; initially this fear will be of accepting the facts about his life. Then he will face the fear of surrendering some of the control—or the appearances of control—that he's held on to for so long.

Once we've become aware of the possibility of surrender, we usually resist it for all we're worth. Confusing surrender with death, loss, and defeat, we struggle against it. This struggle against the inevitable can waste years of our lives. Each of us finds his own way to avoid confronting the fear of surrender. Some people overeat, some use drugs, and others keep themselves too busy to notice the areas of their lives that are falling apart. They fly past the frightening reminders of situations over which they have no control, as if ignoring the truth gave them power over it. It doesn't.

Struggle is a seductive form of resistance, since it gives us such a distinct feeling of "doing something" about our lives. However, if we never stop struggling and ask ourselves what we are struggling *for*, or more specifically what it is we are really trying to resist, we end up like the frightened swimmer thrashing around in the shallow end of the pool, exhausting himself without realizing that if he'd quit swimming so hard he could stand up in the water.

3—*Acknowledging the fear of surrender.* Rather than have an immediate separation, Gene and Carol decide to go to a family therapist. After several sessions with his wife present, Gene goes to a few therapy sessions alone. There he begins to peel away the layers of his fear. (This process of uncovering layers of defensiveness can take months of therapy.) The first fear that comes to mind is the fear of loss—of his home, his wife, his children, the stability of his life, the respect of his friends and neighbors. The most important surrender for him initially is acknowledging the truth about his life at the moment: His primary relationship is on the skids, and his children are unhappy and in trouble. These realizations may trigger other unsettling questions: Does his boss really respect him? Does his secretary really like him? Is he a hopeless failure at everything? At some point he may realize that some part of him had been trying to avoid these questions for a long time.

Gene is not the only one who has a fear of surrender. Look and see: In cases where surrender would not really hurt you, do you fear it? Where is the fear stored in your body? What subjects trigger it in your mind? What feelings and past experiences are associated with it? What would it cost you to give it up? As Frank Herbert writes in *Dune*, "Fear is the mind-killer." It seems that everyone has some fear of surrender; the sooner we acknowledge it, the sooner we can let go of it. We move to the next stage by confronting the fear and cleansing ourselves of it.

4—*Confronting the fear and cleansing ourselves.* A tribe in Africa teaches its children that when a tiger is chasing them in a dream, they should turn and confront the tiger instead of running away from it. In the same way, when we face our fear instead of avoiding it, we may find it is not so ferocious after all.

One night Gene awakens with a jolt. In a dream, he had seen his wife as a giant. She marched him up against a wall and ordered a firing squad to shoot him. Their therapist looked on approvingly. His son and daughter jeered at him as tears streamed down his face. The guards, on orders from his wife, raised their rifles and took aim. Gene wakes up in a cold sweat. He breathes deeply, remembers the dream, and, as his therapist had instructed him, jots it down in a notebook next to his bed.

The image of being up against the wall nags at Gene as he drives to work the next morning, but once absorbed in his duties at the office he manages to shake it off. He gets on with his day. He asks his secretary to type a report. "You know, Gene," she ventures, "I've been meaning to mention to you that some of the other secretaries have been using a different format for this lately, and it seems to be a lot clearer. Would it be okay if I did it that way instead?"

A surge of insane anger runs through his body. He starts to say, "No, dammit, I want you to do it *my* way!" but catches himself in midsentence. Suddenly he is back in his dream of the night before. The guards are about to shoot him; his wife and children are laughing. He blinks and sees his secretary in front of him looking concerned. "Are you all right? I'll do it the way we've always done it if you want me to."

"No, no, go ahead and do what you think best. Could you hold all my calls for the next half hour? I have some work to do."

Alone, he buries his head in his hands. What had triggered such a powerful response? It was just a typing format, after all. Struggling to find the source of his discomfort, he gradually comes to a realization. "I just don't want to be out of control," he says to himself, "and the last few months I feel like everybody's been getting the better of me." The more he thinks about it, the more clearly he sees that the idea of not being in control terrifies him.

By confronting the fear, we take a step toward purging ourselves of it. "The trouble with Westerners is that they do not understand the meaning of the ritual ablutions. It doesn't matter if they are Christians or Moslems, if they are believers in God, then how can they learn to pray without knowing how to wash?" says a tailor in Reshad Feild's *The Last Barrier*.[4] What does it really mean to wash? It means that with effort we remove something that was not really a part of us to begin with. When we wash our bodies, we use soap. The spiritual and psychological soap that helps us wash away our fears and barriers to growth is *awareness* combined with the courage to change. Like Gene, we may find that the initial confrontation with our fear is terrifying. But it is also the beginning of a patient scrubbing that will wash our fears away.

After sharing his dream and his realization with Carol, Gene resolves to keep allowing himself to experience his fears of not being in control. He decides to practice a little surrender.

5—*Conditional surrender (taking a chance)*. Conditional surrenders are the initial experiments we make to discover whether surrender is so awful after all, the small steps we take physically, emotionally, and spiritually to see what happens when we let go instead of holding on.

Gene, after his initial revelations, undertakes his new practice of opening up as a pet project. Like a man entering a cold swimming pool an inch at a time, he starts to take chances with surrender. Still, he never goes in so deep that he couldn't leap back into control in an instant.

He starts with small things. When his wife wants to see the latest sci-fi movie and he wants to see a comedy, he resists the urge to have his way and somewhat graciously agrees to the sci-fi film. His subtle resentment at not seeing his movie is outweighed by the satisfaction he feels about his progress. When his daughter wants to go to an expensive etiquette camp during the summer, he resists the urge to say, "What do you mean? Don't we teach you manners at home?!" and says, "Well, dear, your mother and I will think about it." Then, in line with his new rule of "When in doubt, give in," he agrees. He draws the line at eighty-dollar skateboard wheels for his son.

Gene is not yet comfortable enough with letting go to know whether a restrictive impulse is an appropriate response to the situation at hand or a product of his long-playing record of overcontrol. His life turns into one long bartering session. He'll give in about the catcher's mitt but not about the skateboard; he'll go along with Carol's plans to get a job but not with the suggestion that he cook dinner twice a week. Giving a little here, taking away a little there, he's dancing a fox-trot of control and surrender.

His surrenders seem unnatural and arbitrary, since underlying them is always the attitude that he could still reassert control. Yet they are also valuable, since each time he gives in, he sees that the world does not end. His conditional surrenders familiarize him with the feeling of letting go.

All of us go through periods of conditional surrender in our relationships, opening up a little more to see if the other person will pounce on our vulnerability as we secretly fear. We often act like small children or animals, tentatively approaching a stranger, scurrying for cover if he makes a fast move, and then timidly moving forward to allow ourselves to be touched. Every conditional surrender that brings us closer to others and to our own full potential makes us bold to try the next.

Gene's pleasure at discovering surrender makes him think he should try it more often. His wife and children have mixed feelings about the change in him. They're glad he's changing, but they're so accustomed to having him act like a rock that they sometimes fear he'll go too far. Which is exactly what he does.

6—*Going overboard.* Gene starts reading books on popular psychology and "new age" religion. His own church now seems boring and lacking in true spiritual insight, so he looks for something different. He finds a "spiritually oriented" preacher, one who has thousands of followers all over the country. (Bear in mind that he could have gone overboard in response to any spiritual, religious, or psychological leader—or for no apparent reason at all. This example is not intended as a criticism of preachers.) Gene seems to forget that he had ever been a cautious, controlled person. He does everything the preacher says. This includes making substantial donations to the church, actively proselytizing his colleagues at the office, and generally "surrendering to the will of God" as interpreted by the preacher. His family looks on in shock as he agrees to their most extravagant statements and requests—as long as they do not contradict the preacher's. "No more holding on for me," he says confidently, "I've surrendered."

In his efforts to submit and agree, Gene overlooks the hints of desperation behind this incessant "surrender" and disregards the growing evidence that his obsessive "letting go" is creating harmful fallout in his professional, financial, and family life.

One might be tempted to take Gene aside and tell him that he is not as surrendered as he thinks he is, but he would not understand that now. Gene is going through a pendulum reaction, in which he leaves one polarity (excessive control) and swings to the opposite (excessive surrender) before he can reach a point of balance. With time, love, and a little luck, he will do just that.

Once we have started on a path of conscious surrender, we face the danger of going overboard, of calling an act or feeling "surrender" when in fact it is a product of self-deception or compulsiveness. Some people stay at this stage of development for years, imagining that by "surrendering" to a cult or organization they are showing their great capacity for surrender. While a brief period of overdone surrender seems almost inevitable when we first break free from overcontrol, we need to be wary that it does not become a form of suppression in itself.

For those of us who have been adamantly antisurrender, a little excess surrender might be useful, but only if we do not become as attached to our concepts of surrender as we used to be attached to control. In Gene's case, a meeting with the president of his company rouses him from his overboard reaction. "Gene, you're a great guy, and you've done well for the company for fifteen years now. But if I hear any more complaints from people about your religious trip, I've gotta tell you, I'm going to fire you. Keep your opinions to yourself." The threat of losing his job is like a splash of cold water in the face for Gene—he begins to watch himself more closely. He is heading slowly toward balance.

7—*Balancing.* Any fixed position—whether it's one of control or surrender—becomes deadening after a while. Gene learned through hard experience that his fixation on denial and control did not work. After a while, his over-indulgence in surrender did not work either: It robbed him of his natural autonomy. He gradually comes to realize that he doesn't always *have* to let go: He can choose. The dawn of conscious choice is also the dawn of balance.

One Sunday morning the preacher is in a particularly feisty mood. "Reach into your hearts—and give!" he thunders to the enormous congregation. Gene thinks, "He doesn't mean reach into your hearts—he means reach into your pockets!" One part of him tries to suppress this sacrilegious thought, but another, surer part of him knows that his initial perception was accurate. Before the service ends, he edges his way to the end of the aisle and walks out.

In the days that follow, Gene mulls over the years that had gone by since his wife snapped him out of his unconsciousness by asking for a separation. They are still together, but so many things have changed. He is no longer the closed, rigid man he used to be, and he recognizes that although his stint at oversurrender was good training for him (since it gave him a justification and support system for breaking out of rigidity), that phase is over, too.

"I have to see if I can learn to regulate myself," he thinks. "I ran my life for over forty years before all this started—why should I be doing what someone else tells me now?"

Having explored both ends of the spectrum of compulsive (that is, choiceless) control and surrender, Gene moves into a new period of life: one in which he acts from choice, from an awareness of most of the circumstantial and psychological factors bearing on him. His rational mind and his intuition work together harmoniously. When his children make unreasonable requests, he says no firmly, without fearing that he is falling into an old routine; when they need him to listen without criticism, he can do that too. Sometimes the fearful need to hold on arises again; he's able to see it for what it is and let go of it. For the first time in his life, Gene is a balanced person.

After passing through denial, resistance, and fear, after taking baby steps of surrender and then perhaps going to extremes, we begin to find balance. No longer afraid of anything that suggests surrender, we have the awareness and wisdom to know the difference between surrender that springs from our highest self or (if we believe in God) from God and surrender that is in fact the cloak of self-indulgence or self-deception. We know that compulsiveness, indulgence, and deception will probably be with us all our lives, but we have learned most of their games—and we are less likely to act on their promptings. We learn that we ourselves are the ones who choose, that we ourselves are the only ones who can let go. We re-establish ourselves as active, responsible members of society, endeavoring, as the Zen master Hakuin advised, to experience our enlightenment in the midst of daily life, like the "lotus that blooms from the midst of the fire."

8—*Dynamic surrender in everyday life.* Gene is now fully integrated into his everyday life. He goes to work, makes love with his wife, plays with his children, has long talks with his family and friends, and is generally unrecognizable from the person he was a few years before. There is a serenity about him that makes him attractive to others —somehow they feel better when he's around. His adaptability to the changing needs of every situation, his ability to respond emotionally to people at the level they need most, and his general sense of equanimity make him extraordinary. He is dynamically balanced in his ability to choose both control and surrender.

The greatest test of our surrender *and* of our self-control is everyday life. A moving van pulls out in front of you as you rush to an important appointment—how fluidly do you surrender to the reality of that? Your lover (of the opposite sex) tells you he's realized he's a homosexual—where is your universal tolerance then? You are almost finished with the courses you need to take before entering a new profession, and then the state licensing board changes all the requirements—where is your knowledge of the orderliness of all things? Life is hard. Relationships are hard. There is no avoiding the challenges of survival and success.

In the difficulties that perpetually confront us, we receive countless opportunities to practice dynamic surrender. Daily life, with all its shocks, setbacks, and annoyances, is the ultimate theater in which we play out our dynamic surrender.

STAGES UPON STAGES

Every individual's story of surrender is different. There may not be a preacher or a wife to trigger change as there was for Gene, but circumstances will arrange themselves so that we feel pressed, like the nautilus, to move into ever larger spaces. Of course, there is no guarantee that anyone will move from one stage to the next. Some of us spend our lives in unconsciousness and denial; others move into resistance and stay there forever. Still others may reach a very balanced level with regard to business while staying in unconsciousness and denial about their personal life. Others may freeze up at the first glimpse of fear of letting go and scurry back into the comfort zone of suppression. For those who venture past the monsters of fear and uncertainty that guard the entrance to a path of surrender, the voyage is exciting—still scary at times, but full of wonder and astonishment at how little there was to fear in the first place.

Whether you choose to commit yourself to exploring your potential for dynamic surrender or decide you'd rather sit this lifetime out, rest assured that there will be times when you will surrender and that the stages of surrender will always be open to you when you decide to take the next step. Every stage gives us myriad opportunities to impart form and substance to the spirit of surrender.

12 "SO HOW DO I DO IT?": SURRENDER IN ACTION

Do not permit the events of your daily lives to bind you, but never withdraw yourselves from them. Only by acting thus can you earn the title of a "Liberated One."
—Huang Po

The whole business of self-abandonment is only the business of loving, and love achieves everything.
—Jean-Pierre de Caussade[1]

If you're not having fun, you're not doing it right.
—Anonymous

On April 22, 1984, *The New York Times Magazine*'s lead article focused on Georges Simenon, the celebrated writer of psychological and detective novels. The article stated, "He is reportedly second only to Lenin in being the most widely translated author in the world, having edged out the Bible some years ago. His total worldwide sales are impos-

sible to tally." At age eighty, he said that his interview for
the *Times* would be the last one of his life. Interviewer
Leslie Garis asked him about his creative process:

> "In your *Mémoires*, you write that you put
> yourself into a state of grace before beginning a
> novel. What does that mean?"
> "Vacuum."
> "Vacuum?"
> "When I was very young, in Catholic school,
> we always spoke of *état de grâce*." He intones
> the words with a dramatic ecclesiastical tremor.
> Teresa [his companion] laughs. "I didn't be-
> lieve in it then—the idea of being without sin—
> but I did believe in a sort of vacuum. To me,
> state of grace means being free to receive any
> message. To be completely receptive, you must
> be full of emptiness."

We've already said a lot about surrender—what it is and
isn't, how our resistance to it manifests itself, and the stages
we go through as we deepen our capacity for it. Now we
turn to surrender in action. "Action" is the key, since surrender *is* an act. Every time we enjoy ourselves, we are experiencing some kind of surrender, for the essence of enjoy-
ment is forgetting ourselves for the moment when we reach
for the ball, or run through the surf, or let music carry us
away in rapturous listening or dance, or sit transfixed
through a great movie or play. When we get too caught up
in controlling, we forget that having no control can be *fun*.
Throughout this book we have focused on the positive, expansive aspects of surrender. This expansive aspect is even
more available when we practice surrender in action.

Surrender in action is both simple and difficult—simple
because all it requires is that we get out of the way of life,

and difficult because most of us have an astonishingly powerful resistance to nonresistance. It is tempting to recommend things to *do* to help us surrender, to suggest forms to practice and rules to follow. But while certain activities may induce us to surrender—physical labor, prayer, dance, meditation, singing—they do not guarantee that we will in fact surrender. And paradoxically, most of the time-honored vehicles for surrender, such as prayer and meditation, also require tremendous discipline and control, thus recalling the complementary relationship of surrender and control: Our control frees us to surrender and our surrender enables us to control.

THE FORM DOESN'T MATTER

"I was feeling so lonely a few months after I broke up with my girlfriend," says Charles, "all I could think about was finding someone new. But it seemed like the more I tried to find someone, the less success I had. All the women I met were either involved with someone else, or they weren't attracted to me, or I wasn't attracted to them. It got very depressing. Then I remembered someone once telling me that you never find someone until you let go of the idea of finding someone. That seemed impossible, but I thought about it a lot. One day—it's hard to describe exactly what happened—something shifted inside me, and I found that I felt more comfortable with not having a mate. I actually did 'let go' of that need to find somebody. And you know what happened? The next day I was visiting some friends and this beautiful, unattached woman walked into the room —and into my life."

Our underlying attitude in large part determines whether what we are doing is control or surrender. Are you eating your lunch? Then eat it either with control (counting the calories, judging the cook) or with surrender (with the full awareness of enjoying each bite). Are you making love? You can do it with control (counting your performance minutes, rating your orgasms) or with surrender (for the pure delight of meeting your lover body to body and soul to soul). Are you meditating, or chanting, or following some other form of spiritual practice? You can do it with control (trying to suppress your "evil impulses," using religion to set you apart from or above others) or with surrender (accepting the yoke of your faith with joyous discipline, allowing it to be the vehicle that plunges you into surrender to the divine). You can even read this book with a spirit of control or surrender, either dissecting and judging every point or exercising an open mind that enables you to use what works and freely let go of anything that doesn't pertain to your life.

We don't need any special equipment to surrender, just our spirit and an open heart. When we are offered a better job at a higher salary, we may waver before accepting, wondering if we are worthy or if the added responsibilities are worth the risk. By taking a chance on it, we actively surrender to the opportunity of the moment. When a new love appears to take the place of the stolid aloneness we've constructed, there is a moment of doubt—should I give up my equilibrium for the uncertainty of sharing my life? We can actively surrender to the adventure of love.

Despite our occasional descents into the quagmires of overcontrol, we can dynamically surrender anytime, streaming unencumbered through an instant of life, acting without a divided mind. Whether in the form of nonaction, allowing situations to play themselves out, or of action, single-mindedly spinning across a dance floor, surrender is here, now, an acceptance of life.

LETTING CIRCUMSTANCES PLAY THEMSELVES OUT

"When my husband and I found out I was pregnant," says Deborah, a textile representative in Philadelphia, "we were shocked—and not very happy. His job was in jeopardy and I had just decided to start a new business. It didn't seem like very good timing. But now Andrew is two, and he is the most wonderful addition to our lives we could ever have imagined. And I'm going ahead with my business plans now. I'm glad we let it work out the way we did."

Even in life-changing situations less consequential than having a child, letting things play themselves out can work in our best interest. "After months of house hunting, we found a house that looked so perfect for us that I wanted it immediately," says Nancy, manager of a health club in Brentwood, California. "A few years ago I would have really pushed to make sure I got it, but this time was different. I did everything I could to get it—filled out the rental application, met with the landlord, and got my references in promptly. At the same time my attitude was that if it was meant to be ours, we'd get it, and if not, we'd find something better. As it turned out, I realized that it really wasn't right for me, even though it was beautiful. The landlord offered it to us, and we actually turned it down. I don't think I could have gone through that process so smoothly and made the decision that was ultimately best if I hadn't been willing to let the situation develop instead of rushing in to manage it."

Letting situations play themselves out does not mean standing in the middle of the freeway to see what will happen. When it is time to act, we must act. But there are times when the best action is *non*action. In Tolstoy's *War*

and Peace, an old general counsels young Prince Andrei
about the power of timely nonaction:

> "It's not very difficult to take a fortress: what is
> difficult is to win a campaign. And for that it's
> not storming and attacking that are wanted, but
> *patience and time.* Kamensky dispatched soldiers
> to Rustchuk, but I dispatched only them—
> patience and time—and I took more fortresses
> than he did. . . ."
> "But we shall have to accept battle, shall we
> not?" asked Prince Andrei.
> "Very likely. If that's what everybody wants,
> then there's no help for it. . . . But believe me,
> my boy, there is no more powerful adversary
> than those two: patience and time—they will
> do it all. . . . I'll tell you what to do, and what
> I do. When in doubt, my dear fellow—," he
> paused, "do nothing."[2]

"Nothing" can be very hard to do. When we do nothing,
events take their own course. The principle of timely nonaction is summed up in the ancient Chinese oracle *I Ching.*
In the section "Keeping Still," it says, "When it is time to
stop, then stop; when the times comes for action, then act!
By choosing activity and stillness, each at the proper time,
a man achieves glorious progress." In some cases inaction is
our most dynamic surrender. If we don't know whether our
situation requires the surrender of letting things be or the
surrender of plunging in wholeheartedly, we can begin by
remembering the old general's advice: When in doubt, do
nothing. Let it be.

PASSIONATE DISPASSION:
NONATTACHMENT TO RESULTS

It is permissible to take life's blessings with both
hands provided you know yourself prepared in
the opposite event to take them just as gladly.
—Meister Eckhart

We can put everything we have into getting a job, or making
a specific amount of money, or having a relationship with
a particular person, and at the same time realize that if we
don't get it, it ultimately does not matter. We will go on to
something else. We can passionately lay heart, mind, and
time on the line and know that if it doesn't work out, it's
fine. Our actions may *appear* the same as if we were trying
frantically to control—we might make the same phone calls
to try to have our way, give the same speeches, and so forth
—but the *spirit* behind them is different. We are ultimately
dispassionate about the outcome. Feelings of disorder and
insecurity are diminished, and we are at least as likely to
end up getting what we wanted anyway.

Harvey Harrison, a veteran of many negotiations, com-
mented to me, "Many times a good negotiator will not
achieve everything in a deal he wants. Sometimes things just
work out that way. I think that over time, negotiators who
really understand the art of negotiating develop certain
goals, and a major goal really, rather than winning any
particular point in a negotiation, is to develop mastery.
What happens is after a while you stop having concern for
any specific outcome, although of course you always do your
best and you try to make the best deal you can. It becomes
not so much a question of whether you can win this particular negotiated point with this particular counterpart as
a question of whether you understood what was going on
objectively, whether you understood your counterpart,

whether you said the things you should have said in the way and at the time you should have said them, and whether you didn't say the things you shouldn't have said. When you're not so attached to the result, you are dealing with it from a standpoint of mastery."

GETTING PHYSICAL:
AN OPPORTUNITY FOR SURRENDER

> Somebody asked the master, Bokuju, "We have to dress and eat every day—how do we get out of all that?" Bokuju answered, "We dress, we eat." The questioner said, "I don't understand." Bokuju answered, "If you don't understand, put on your clothes and eat your food."
> —Zen kōan

Although any activity can be an occasion for dynamic surrender, physical activity is a great vehicle for it. Whether we are raking the leaves, hammering a nail, typing a letter, carving a roast, or riding a bicycle, every physical action gives us the opportunity to fully lose ourselves in it. Of course, we don't *have* to use our actions as opportunities for dynamic surrender. We can use them to separate ourselves from what we are doing, to lose focus, feel scattered, and act with resistance and control. The choice is ours, moment by moment. But by using every act to focus ourselves absolutely and abandon ourselves to the craft of action— cutting that celery stalk perfectly or driving in that nail with total concentration—we continually refine our capacity for surrender. Perfect focus and perfect abandonment are not contradictory: The more clearly we focus, the more we can give ourselves to what we are doing. We can learn to relieve ourselves of the burden of self-consciousness and vanish for a moment into the activity at hand.

The Zen tradition is full of stories of students who reached full enlightenment while working or performing some simple action. Reverend Gensho Fukushima, Abbot of Hofukuji, the largest Zen monastery in Kyoto, Japan, told me that he reached full *satori*, or awakening, while picking up a fork. Through work we can experience all levels of surrender, from the most primitive to the most exalted. If we work distractedly, we'll be lucky to surrender even to the extent of turning on the oven before putting in the cake or putting the tape in the dictating machine before dictating our letter. As concentration on our work increases, our chances of moving toward complete surrender to the moment increase.

OVERCOMING PAIN THROUGH SURRENDER

> Do not try to drive pain away by pretending it is not real; pain, if you seek serenity in Oneness, will vanish of its own accord.
> —Seng Ts'an

> Remember that the rose bush can produce a perfect rose only through correct pruning. The pruning may hurt the plant temporarily, but if the plant were able to understand the necessity, then it would be filled with joy each time the gardener came with the knife.
> —Reshad Feild[3]

When we're having fun we often experience surrender without realizing it. Hours fly by when we're watching a good movie, or absorbed in a great basketball game, or laughing with someone we love. It's the quality of not planning, resisting, and worrying that *makes* fun fun. What we do not always realize is that we can carry that same spirit of relaxation and lightness into experiences that we usually consider decidedly not fun.

Coping with physical pain offers us other opportunities to master dynamic physical surrender. When we are in pain, we have a tendency to tense up. We wish it weren't there. It frightens us, so we brace ourselves to keep from feeling it. But the more effort we put into resisting or denying it, the stronger it usually becomes. "I had a throbbing headache," says Warren, a copywriter at a major advertising firm. "It had gone on for hours; I'd taken all the medicine I dared to and nothing seemed to help. Then I noticed that I was so intent on getting rid of the pain of the headache that I was making myself more tense just to keep from feeling it. I forced myself to relax and focus *into* it rather than away from it. I remembered an exercise I'd learned— about describing exactly how the pain looked, what size and texture it was, and so on, and I was amazed to find that within a few minutes of looking into it, the headache was gone."

Ann, a literary agent in San Francisco, remembers overcoming her fear and pain in the dental chair by surrendering to it. "If I get a shot of Novocain, I feel ill for days. A few months ago I had to have a crown removed and a temporary crown put on. The dentist started to prepare the anesthetic, and I told her I didn't want it. Instead, I focused my mind throughout the procedure on letting the pain flow out freely from every pore in my body. She had to drill down the base of the tooth under the old crown and fit the new one, but I kept on visualizing my whole body letting go of the pain, letting it flow out and away. It worked so well that my dentist has started recommending it to other patients who don't want Novocain." The next time you are suffering from physical pain, go into it instead of away from

it. You may find that the best way to control pain is to surrender to it.

Any experience that pushes us to a new level of intensity
can trigger us to surrender. Crisis precipitates surrender
because it catapults us beyond our previous limits whether
we like it or not. The mother who somehow musters the
strength to lift a car off her child trapped beneath, the
atheist who find God after a near-death experience, the
businessman who changes his lifestyle after a heart attack—
all these people are forced by circumstances to see their lives
and their capacities in a completely new way.

In *The Perennial Philosophy*, an examination of the
commonality of all the world's mystical traditions, Aldous
Huxley points out that one of the distinguishing factors of
sainthood is the realization that *every* experience can be
seen as the "crisis" that triggers us to new levels of perception. He writes: "The saint is one who knows that every
moment of our human life is a moment of crisis; for at
every moment we are called upon to make an all-important
decision—to choose between the way that leads to death
and spiritual darkness and the way that leads to light and
life; . . . between our personal will, or the will of some projection of our personality, and the will of God."[4]

The origin of the word "crisis" is the Greek *krisis*, meaning "decision." Crisis precipitates decision. Seeing life as a
perpetual "crisis" that makes us choose the path of life over
the path of death helps us appreciate both the frailty and
the glory of life. It also helps us understand personal crises
in a broader perspective. But the lessons we learn from
crisis are painful, and we would rarely choose them for
ourselves.

"If someone had come to me a few months ago and said,
'The child you are carrying will be stillborn, and after the
emergency delivery you will be unable to have any more

children, but as a result of this you will find new meaning
in your life and develop greater depth, sensitivity and compassion—are you willing to do this?' I would have said,
'No, let me have the baby and I'll stay the way I am," says
Joanne a few months after her experience. "I would never
have gone through this voluntarily, but I do see that every
great tragedy of my life has returned me to the source of
life and the source of compassion far more intensely than
I would ever have pushed myself." The most practical way
to get "surrender value" from crisis is this: Don't look for
crises, but if one comes, ask yourself what decisions you can
make to surrender the shell of your old life and expand—
transformed—into the new.

Sickness is another unpopular but potent teacher of surrender. Betty, an attractive woman in her early thirties, was
working on a sailboat a few years ago when she collapsed
and began a nightmare of mysterious illness. She was given
up for dead more than once as she lay emaciated and full
of intravenous needles alone in a hospital, far from her
family and friends. In discussing the "surrender lessons" she
learned from this, she says, "I didn't want to admit that I
didn't feel right, so I kept working until I almost died.
Once I got really ill, I was in the hospital and I had no
control at all. I had to surrender to the fact that I was really
sick, and allow all kinds of medical procedures to be per-
formed on my body. It was a very difficult lesson, but I feel
I grew a lot from going through it." Those who are willing
to use illness as a laboratory of applied surrender often
emerge strengthened and cleansed.

Surrendering to the fact of illness is an essential step in
physical recovery, for as long as we insist that nothing is
wrong, our illness will remain untreated. Once we have
accepted the reality of our problem, even more challenging
lessons in surrender remain: surrendering to competent
medical treatment, allowing ourselves to be on the receiving

end of love and care, and giving up the goals and plans that had recently seemed so important, all in order to devote ourselves to healing our body and mind.

One of the reasons suffering, crisis, and sickness offer such profound lessons in surrender is that until we are forced into surrender by some great misfortune, we tend to continue our efforts to control; we resist surrender without realizing how much we could gain if we surrendered to life (with all its pleasure and excitement) *without* being forced into it by catastrophe. Why do we wait until surrender is our only option? When confronted with undeniable crisis, we may try to surrender gracefully, but only after exhausting every possibility to keep on controlling. Instead of letting go our rigid points of view, we hold on until, like bandits holed up in a house surrounded by SWAT teams, we pipe up in midcrisis, "Surrender! What a good idea!"

In line with the time-honored tradition of quitting before one is fired, I suggest finding pleasant—or at least novel—ways of dynamically surrendering before surrender becomes our final, crisis-linked option.

SURRENDER BREAKS: MORE REFRESHING THAN COFFEE

> Happiness runs in a circular motion,
> Thought is like a little boat upon the sea,
> Everybody is a part of anything anyway,
> You can have everything if you let yourself be.
> —Donovan[5]

Management consultant R. G. H. Siu, author of *The Craft of Power* and *Transcending the Power Game: The Way to Executive Serenity*, spoke to me from his home in Washington, D.C. "I suggest to many of my clients that they regularly take short breaks just to relax and let things be. Whether it's an hour spent sitting on the back porch listening to the birds sing or a brisk walk through the park, they invariably return to the office refreshed, better able to resonate with the people around them and more prepared to make sound business decisions." Carrying this wise advice a step further, I suggest that each of us create "surrender breaks" in the midst of our daily lives—periods set aside for the sole purpose of letting go the concerns, thoughts, and plans that have been plaguing us, periods for just "being there" in the moment with no concern for the past or future.

It is easier to get into the mood for a surrender break if we take a few moments at the beginning to become aware of our breath. Take several deep breaths, focus on letting go whatever is on your mind, and let yourself be. People who find it difficult to sit still without doing something can take their surrender breaks by walking (not running—that usually devolves into a goal-oriented form of work), puttering in a garden, playing with children, going to a ball game, or engaging in some noncompetitive sport.

The more reflective (or sedentary, depending on your point of view) may prefer to practice some form of meditation, or simply to sit in the sun or in front of the fireplace (the heater maybe?) thinking about nothing. Of course, thoughts will buzz through the mind no matter how much nothing we're thinking about—what makes this period of nondoing special is that we let the thoughts fly by without chasing after them. In the course of half an hour in the garden, thousands of images may float through the mind— of projects undone, relationships in progress, bills not paid, memories of the past, and dreams of the future. This is natural.

During a surrender break, however, we let these images run through without turning them into a train of thought.

They come and they go, like clouds wafting across the sky. "Clouds, my foot!" you might reply, "I don't want to waste my time doing nothing!" This attitude, which is encouraged in all of us by society's high priority on "doing" things, betrays ignorance about the true source of productivity: Creation begins when something meets nothing. Without the "nothing" of open space, we cannot add anything new. Time spent "doing nothing" is, in fact, the most creative time we spend all day. It's a tribute to the power of letting go our usual commotion of consciousness that twenty or thirty minutes of a surrender break can energize us for many hours of activity. Even a five-minute break, a walk around the block, or a few minutes spent staring out at the horizon can return us to our work and our relationships with renewed perspective, energy, and enthusiasm. Try it.

PRAYER AND SURRENDER TO GOD

Who hath resisted Him, and hath had peace?
—Job 9:4

To surrender to God is to practice every virtue.
—Jean-Pierre de Caussade[6]

The prayer of which I speak is the prayer of the heart, the state where all life has become a prayer.
—Reshad Feild[7]

For many people, the ultimate surrender is to God, a surrender often facilitated through prayer.

When we surrender to our business, to relationships, or to our material or physical desires, we often get more of what we surrendered to—more power, more money, perhaps more love from other people. And this is fine. But both mortal and material prizes are inherently limited, inherently transitory. Surrender to something limited, such as a job or even a relationship, is limited by the boundaries of whatever is surrendered to.

Is there a force or presence great enough to hold *total* surrender? Those who believe in God feel that only the divine is vast and loving enough for that. If we surrender to unlimitedness, then the possibilities for expanding ourselves through surrender are also unlimited—or at least they are bounded only by our own limitations. As the religious philosopher Sören Kierkegaard wrote, "There was one who conquered everything by his power, and there was one who conquered God by his powerlessness. There was one who relied upon himself and gained everything; there was one who in the security of his own strength sacrificed everything; but the one who believed God was the greatest of all."[8]

Not all those who believe in God feel comfortable with the concept of prayer; those who see no value in it obviously need not pray. Clearly, this is a matter of intimate personal choice, and those who find their most powerful experiences of God in the face of someone they love, or in the pounding of the sea, or in the blooming of a flower are practicing their religion in the way that suits them best. Nevertheless, in every culture and every major religious tradition on earth there appears some form of prayer—supplication to a benevolent and all-knowing force with the hope of obtaining guidance and, sometimes, material assistance. Devoted prayer seeks to effect the deepest intimacy with the divine.

As with all other actions, the nature of prayer changes according to the state of mind of the one who is praying. If a person prays with a spirit of control, he is still fixated on control; but if he prays with a spirit of surrender, he opens himself to whatever is available through surrender to God. If he prays to have his desires fulfilled, he has abandoned neither his sense of ego nor his attachment to what that ego wants. When we attempt to use prayer as a vehicle for satisfying our ego needs, we risk deceiving ourselves about the virtuousness of our intentions.

There is always the temptation to confuse our personal desires with what we are sure God would want for us if He were speaking to us personally. "I'm sure God wouldn't mind my charging this personal expense to my business credit card. In fact, I probably wouldn't even want to if it weren't part of His divine plan." Nice try. If our impulse to "surrender to God" leads us to abandon our moral code, family, job, and community responsibilities, we had better doubt its divine inspiration. (Murderers, after all, have used "God" as a justification for their crimes; this is perhaps the most patent example of deluded and life-negating surrender.) The possibilities for self-deception in prayer and surrender to God do not, however, negate the vast potential of this type of active surrender.

For most people, surrender to God does not just "happen." One *chooses* to do it, but its manifestation can be either passive or active. The decision to "let go and let God" is a choice to set aside one's personal will so that the divine will can manifest itself unimpeded. The decision to consciously work at clearing away the psychological and emotional barriers that block one's perception of God is a choice to harness one's will for the same purpose. In either case the goal is the same: heightened perception of the divine and cooperation with the divine will.

PRACTICING DYNAMIC SURRENDER

Theoretically, the benefits of creating "space" through surrender—letting things play themselves out or giving yourself up to the moment—may be clear. In practice, however, it's often not easy to just "let go." We hate our job; we've been looking for a new one for months and there's not a lead on the horizon. We know it may be time to back off a little, but we still want the job. Or we are lonely; we want new friends, or a mate. We may know that the best way to find someone is to let go of the notion that we need a companion. But we are still alone, and we still don't like it. "Just let go," advise our happily employed and mated friends. "Nothing will happen until you do." But the times when we most *need* to let go are also the times when we least *want* to.

"Letting go" is not a physical action; it is a mental shift. The extent to which we can even "decide" to let go is limited, since the very urgency of a desire to let go blocks surrender from taking place. In his final book, Alan Watts summed up this problem: "If I desire not to desire, is that not already desire? How can I desire not to desire? How can I surrender myself when myself is precisely an urge to hold on, to cling . . . ?"[9]

As we sit in our living room, office, or car, wishing, longing, praying for a break, feeling the constriction of our own neediness and desire, and knowing that little will happen until we let go of it, there *are* a few things we can do to make that shift into dynamic surrender. The first is to *notice the desire*—for love, friends, money, the resolution to a problem, or whatever. See how strong that desire is. The second step is to *notice the sense of false incompletion or imperfection from which the desire springs*. Urgent desires to have things, people, or situations spring from an underlying feeling that something is currently lacking. But in fact the world is overflowing with agreeable people and abundance we could have near us if we'd quit blocking their approach. The third step is to begin to *step outside the desire.* At the moment we are consumed with it, the desire may seem to fill every atom of our being, but in actuality the desire is *not* all we are. It is something we have and therefore something we can set aside. The fourth and final step is to *release.* This usually follows the third step spontaneously, provided we do not block it. Release is a mental shift, as a result of which the job or the companion (or whatever it was) no longer appears as all-important, but as just what it is: a job, or a companion, or a "whatever." This detachment from the sense of all-consuming need opens the space for surrender—and for creation.

No matter how rigidly controlled you are or have been, you have already practiced surrender. Every time you see and accept a situation as it is—even if that only means staying in bed when you know you have the flu—you are showing your capacity for surrender. Every time you let yourself laugh or cry, you are allowing yourself to surrender. In fact, most of the peak experiences of life include surrender. Surrender is already with us, and we can decide to go with it instead of against it. Consciously practicing surrender in action means deciding to let things go and to let them be. The more willing we are to let things go—or to throw ourselves without restraint into the possibilities of the moment—the more exuberantly alive we feel.

All that's necessary is to use the capacity for surrender inside us right now. The same surrender that makes the most enjoyable moments so enjoyable can be applied in any situation. Work or play, happiness or sadness, all can be experienced in a spirit of surrender. Whatever you are doing, or must do, abandon yourself to it. This means abandoning yourself to the way things are. Identify the facts and then fling yourself into your activity; dance with it, dive into it, jump for it, go for it, and enjoy it. Life is not heavy or onerous when we approach it with an attitude of dynamic surrender. Even suffering becomes easier to bear when we perceive it as an opportunity for surrender.

Sweet, sweet surrender is truly satisfying and joyful. In its simplest form, dynamic surrender is saying yes instead of no—to whatever happens. And nothing happens until someone says yes.

13 *SURRENDER TO OTHERS: WIN OR LOSS?*

Surrender yourself humbly; then you can be
trusted to care for all things.
Love the world as your own self; then you can
truly care for all things.
                              —*Tao te Ching*

Only don't keep on refusing for the sake of refusing. It's an exercise of power; but accepting's
after all an exercise of power as well.
                              —Henry James,
                              The Portrait of a Lady

"When I met Leo, he said it was okay with him if we didn't
have a 50-50 relationship, that he could deal with 60-40,"
says Madeleine, a public relations consultant in Beverly
Hills. "I thought, 'This is great—I've finally met a real
man, somebody who doesn't have to be in control all the
time.' It never occurred to me that the 60 percent wouldn't
be mine." Madeleine's husband, who owns a fashionable
shoe store, says, "We fought terribly for the first two years
of our marriage, each of us trying to get the upper hand."

"That's right," says Madeleine, "I participated in fights that, in looking back, I cannot believe I was there for. We went through two sets of dishes before it got too expensive to keep throwing them." After two years of conflict, Madeleine and Leo realized that they loved each other too much to separate, but they would be fighting for the rest of their lives if they didn't find a different way. "We had to work through every major issue in our lives and struggle through 'my way' and 'your way' until we got to 'our way,'" says Leo. "Now both of us know that the only way to deal with each other is with love. If she comes to me and says, 'Honey, could you take care of this for me?' I'll do it in a minute, but if she comes on with that 'Leo, do this,' attitude, I just say, 'Come on—we've been through that one before.' Then she says, 'Oh, I was just kidding,' and we move on."

"I wanted to acquire the film rights to a best-selling novel and work on the movie with an established movie producer whom I'd been friends with for years," says Judith, a screenwriter in New York. "When I first talked to him about it, he said, 'I'll go ahead with it, but you need to know that you will have no control once the project starts.' I agreed, because he was putting up the money and this was my first big project, but I didn't really give up the idea of having some creative control. As soon as the rights were bought, I found I wanted more and more control over the screenplay and the casting, and it began to bother me. We started exchanging nasty letters about broken agreements and got our lawyers involved. Soon our relationship had deteriorated to the point that we were ready to sue each other. My lawyer called me and said, 'Judith, just stop. You cannot win this one.' So I decided to let the whole thing go. It was a struggle for me to give up my attachment to having 'my' project turn out the way I wanted it to, but

I'd gotten myself into a no-win situation. For the first time, I really did give the control to Jeffrey, my friend.

"What's been most amazing to me is that the moment I stopped trying to bulldoze him into doing things my way, I began to get more control. We weren't locked into this adversarial battle, so we could be friends again and talk about the book and the film. Several major creative decisions—about the lead actors and the score of the movie—have gone the way I wanted them to, and it's all happened since I quit pushing."

What does it mean to surrender to another person? Is it the same as denying ourselves, knuckling under, and submitting? Surrender to others can be either healthy or destructive. It depends on the situation. Surrender in a business context may taken the form of delegating responsibility to a trusted subordinate, but it can also mean going out of business or being taken over by an unfriendly competitor. Surrender is essential to falling in love, giving unselfishly, and maintaining strong relationships of all kinds, including those between parent and child, between husband and wife, and between friends. If we are unwilling to surrender, we will not allow ourselves to be vulnerable, to give, and to compromise. Relationships, particularly intimate ones, are the most challenging testing grounds for our ability to surrender dynamically and positively because there our fear of merging with another person or losing our strength through submission is strongest.

In commercial terms, it is certainly possible to lose out to a competitor, but this is not usually due to surrender, unless we are forced into bankruptcy or accepting a takeover. Discussing control and surrender in the library of his home in Princeton, New Jersey, George Ball, the veteran diplomat, points out: "Rarely is anyone in a situation where surrender need mean complete surrender. It can occur, but it doesn't often occur. Therefore, anyone who is in a very difficult position, faced with having to decide whether to fight on untenable terrain, has to look at what the other options are, what the alternatives are, what the consequences would be, how to limit damage, all of these things. Rarely is a person faced with a situation where a decision to give up necessarily means total capitulation. It may happen in a situation involving military force, but not in normal human affairs, in politics, or in business."

Even when surrender to others really is loss or defeat, it does not mean that we will ultimately end up any worse off than we would have been if we'd "won." If our surrender in relationships is damaging us, then we are practicing life-negating surrender; we need to let go of the relationship or change it. Surrender itself need only be a defeat when we choose to make it so.

KNOW YOURSELF: THE BASIS OF SURRENDER TO OTHERS

How can we surrender to another if we are not first clear about who *we* are? Unless we have a personal sense of strength and confidence, what we think is surrender to another is more likely to be a mushy combination of our own insecurities and someone else's. Surrender to another is not dependency, nor is it submission. It is consciously giving ourselves, and we cannot *give* ourselves unless we first *have* ourselves. Only a general who is really in control of his army can order it to surrender; if his troops have already mutinied, his declaration of surrender is meaningless. Only if we are strong within ourselves can we *choose* surrender. Personal strength and self-knowledge are prerequisites of surrender to another.

KNOW WHO YOU ARE
SURRENDERING TO

"I've always been a firm believer in commitment," says Martin, a physician, "and when I married my wife I intended to stay with her no matter what. After a few years I saw how hard that would be. She used to fly into uncontrollable rages, and then if I talked about a separation, she'd fall apart. Once she pulled a gun on me, and another time I had to leave my office in the middle of the day to go home and take a .38 out of her hand to keep her from killing herself. I hated to see our son watching it all. This went on for fifteen years; I was so dogged about it that I thought if we could just work on it a little longer, if she would just find the right therapist, the marriage would work out. Finally, I realized that the relationship would never work because she didn't really want it to—and that maybe she couldn't make it work. If she had been willing or able to change, she would have, but I couldn't spend the rest of my life—not to mention our son's life—waiting for her to get around to it. Now I regret that I didn't see the futility of the situation and get out of it long before I did."

Besides knowing ourselves before surrendering to another, it's important that we know who that other person is. Without awareness of the other person's character and needs, how can we know if our surrender is appropriate? How can we know if he is interested in being surrendered to? How can we give to another person—whether we are giving time, gifts, or ourselves—if we don't know who he is? All surrender begins with the acceptance of facts. Surrender to others begins with accepting others as they are—fears, nasty tendencies, idiosyncrasies and all. Once we know whom we are dealing with, we know if they are willing and able to surrender to us, and we can choose whether to control, to get them out of our lives, or to surrender.

As part of our surrender to reality, we have to determine when it would be a waste of time and energy for us to develop a relationship with a particular person. With someone who is almost certain to sabotage or betray us, the most appropriate choice is to walk away. We must let go of our desire to have that person be someone he is not.

As Judith Mishell, a clinical psychologist, says, "Giving begins with knowledge—knowledge of ourselves and knowledge of the other person." Our relationships have a realistic basis when we recognize the full spectrum of characteristics within the person before us. Essential to this realism is the knowledge that ultimately we cannot control or change the person. Seeing people as they actually are can be difficult, since it involves setting aside our dreams of having our fantasies fulfilled. Yet it is crucial to our own health and the health of our relationships.

"I kept thinking that one day my husband would come home from work with a huge bouquet of roses and say, 'Jeannie, I love you more than anything else in the world,' " says the wife of an aerospace executive. "Since he never *said* 'I love you' or showed it in ways that *I* thought were meaningful, I always had a nagging feeling that he didn't really love me. This plagued me for years. Then we went away for a marriage encounter weekend, and I told him what I was feeling. He was so shocked, and so hurt. 'Why would I have stayed with you all these years if I didn't love you?' he asked. As we talked it over, I realized that he actually *had* been communicating that he loved me through gestures and through being there, but in ways I had been unwilling to accept." People are not always going to express themselves or behave in our favorite ways; by putting ourselves in their position and developing a sense of how their minds operate, we become able to accept them on their own terms.

SURRENDER AS LOSS: GIVING IN

"My boss could not let a day go by without putting me down for something," says Anna. "I thought that part of my job was to be open to feedback—and to put up with a certain amount of aggravation—so I never fought back. But the fact was that he was only one rung above me on the corporate ladder, and I wasn't doing such a bad job. I let him beat me down every day until I really started feeling like a worthless old dust mop." Anna was not surrendering to her boss in a life-serving way. She was submitting to psychological abuse in a way that damaged her self-esteem.

Lest we overlook the traditional meanings of surrender, let's look at surrender that in fact represents the ignominious betrayal of one's principles and the abdication of a cherished position. In short, defeat. Just as military surrender connotes loss, so a life-negating surrender on a person-to-person level feels like humiliating capitulation. When we surrender to another by succumbing to that person's greater power or influence, we are surrendering in the least exalted sense.

A key distinguishing factor between surrender to another as joyful expansion and surrender as subjugation or defeat is *mutuality*. There is a distinct difference between subordination which makes one feel smaller (as when a wife sacrifices her own needs for the sake of her husband or children until she feels there is nothing left of herself) and subordination which comes from the self-confidence and strength of knowing that we can give to another person without diminishing ourselves. If a wife accepts her husband and adapts to his character, but the husband insists on freezing her into a rigid role and doing everything his way, her so-called surrender is really subjugation, a bondage she has accepted. Dynamic surrender goes both ways: I surrender to you and you surrender to me.

DELEGATION AS DYNAMIC SURRENDER

In the interviews I conducted for this book, one sentiment emerged over and over: The best way to control people is to let them go. In business, this means finding people you trust and respect, and letting them go within the structure of your organization. Malcolm Forbes summed this up when he said, "Nobody can enjoy what they're doing if somebody's looking over their shoulder or holding them in. You've got to let somebody out if you want to get the full measure. People can only enjoy themselves if they have some responsibility. You keep control only by having confidence in those you give responsibility to and letting them exercise it. By giving away control, you keep it." (This is true in personal relationships as well. The husband who is not threatened when his wife spends an evening with friends has a happier spouse at the end of the evening; the child who knows his parents trust him to do his homework feels more personal pride and satisfaction when he spurs himself to do it without prompting; the woman who is not jealous of her best friend's other friends finds her own social world expanded when her friend introduces her to others.)

Even businessmen who are obsessed with retaining ultimate control of their enterprise learn to allow others to do their jobs if they want to get ahead. As Malcolm Forbes told me, "The man who makes himself indispensable cannot be promoted or grow greater, because who'll do his job if he's the only one that can or thinks he can? To keep being indispensable is to cut off your future. You stay in control by having people who don't need a tight rein but who can do the job they're paid to do better than you could do it." Michael Fuchs, president of Home Box Office, sat back in an armchair in his suite at the Beverly Hills Hotel and said that he learned this through experience: "I would say that I have inevitably had to surrender a lot of control. When I started at HBO I hadn't worked at a corporation, and for the first year I thought my role was to have as few people working for me as possible and to do everything myself. It took me a long time to be talked into realizing that it's an organization that the company wants. That became a particular joy to me, building an organization. I was in charge of business affairs; I surrendered business affairs. I was in charge of sports; I surrendered sports. I was in charge of original programming; I surrendered that. What became important to me was not necessarily controlling a particular department. What was important was controlling the overall direction—it's like being the captain. That means I had to surrender the details, some of which are very gratifying and involving. I think its a worthwhile trade-off."

Letting other people excel at what was previously your job brings out the best in them and also allows you to expand your horizons. Vidal Sassoon, who oversees a multi-million-dollar beauty and cosmetics empire, says, "I sense that building, creating, is a team effort. Very early on, I built my team around me, and many of them took over parts of what I did at one time and did it better than I did.

It felt marvelous to me. When I left England and came to New York, my attitude was that I had built a first-class team and I had to test it, and there was absolutely no turning back. I had to go to New York and do what I did. And you know what happened? The original team that I left in England did better without me." In a similar vein Michael Fuchs states, "I have tried to find very strong people to work with me. I think it's very important that they be out front and have authority over their organizations. Yet I'm the one who has to bear in mind the overall direction of the company and ask the key questions. Anything anyone who works for me can do better than me, as well as me, or almost as well as me and feels strongly about doing, that is something I let him do."

If a manager delegates grudgingly, allowing someone else to do a job only because he has reluctantly admitted that he is unable to supervise the warehousemen and still oversee the direction of his company, then his attitude is still one of restriction and control. His staff will sense this and is likely to respond the way most people do when they feel they are not being trusted to do what they are trained and paid for: with covert resentment and diminished productivity. But when a manager delegates with a spirit of surrender, employees know what is expected of them and enjoy the freedom of doing their job without the boss's intrusive presence. Jay Olins, founder and president of the multimillion-dollar California Student Loan Finance Corporation, says, "I am happiest when I have people working with me, or for me, who are really capable of handling their responsibilities and leaving me time to pursue my broader corporate and personal goals. Then I tend to keep out of what they are doing except to look at it occasionally." Michael Fuchs summarizes in-house corporate surrender this way: "One of my favorite expressions in terms of running an organization is 'You work for them more than they [the employees] work for you.'" In true delegation, both employees and employers win.

Successful business leaders know that it is better to give the people working around them the freedom to rise. They recognize that through this surrender to others they increase corporate productivity, improve morale, and open the way for their own rise to greater heights of personal success.

SERVICE: THE GIVER RECEIVES

No matter what it is, if a man is afraid of losing it, he will lose it, but if he is willing to give it up, he will get it. So be ready to give up your life for the good of the people around you.
—Toyo Tenshitsu

One of our most significant conclusions about excellent companies is that, *whether their basic business is metal bending, high technology, or hamburgers, they have all defined themselves as service businesses.*
—Thomas J. Peters
and Robert H. Waterman, Jr.,
In Search of Excellence[1]

Delegation is one form of in-house surrender to others: management's surrender of responsibility and trust to staff. Another form of corporate surrender takes place in the relationship between the company and the public. That form is *service*.

Many of us think that service is something to complain

about in restaurants. Or we might see it as something that only servants (janitors, cleaning ladies, and so forth) do. But service has a much broader meaning. Here it is defined as a form of surrender *to*, in which we act solely for the other person's benefit without thought of ourselves. For hundreds of years it was accepted that public service, whether volunteering for philanthropic organizations, giving time and money to the needy, or participating in the nation's political process, was an essential part of every citizen's life. It is still an integral part of the lives of millions of people. "The way I was reared was that you started with 'do your thing, be your own person,' but only if that led you from the microcosm to the macrocosm," says Barbara Boyle of Orion Pictures. "Nothing was done so that there would be personal gratification or aggrandizement. It really had to do with becoming something so that you could give back." Successful businesses recognize that of all their divisions, service is perhaps the most important. IBM has built its corporate image around the concept "IBM means service." Frito-Lay has captured and maintained an enormous share of the snack-foods market not only by making crunchier corn chips but also by maintaining a service force that will brave blizzards to deliver its product, even to the smallest accounts. The company knows that customers appreciate service and that happy customers buy again.

Particularly in this era of burgeoning computer and information technology, businesses of all sizes realize that the sales power of the future lies in service. John Naisbitt, author of *Megatrends*, describes "high tech/high touch" as a major contemporary trend. "High tech" means all those machines that seem to work miracles; "high touch" is the heightened degree of personal attention that we need as we accustom ourselves to the presence of these gizmos in

our daily lives. Our economy is shifting away from com-
modities into the service and information sectors. Understanding the deeper meaning of service will therefore be
profitable as well as personally valuable in years to come.

One advantage of serving others is that when we extend
ourselves for others, they are more inclined to extend themselves for us. Consider the following incident recounted in
In Search of Excellence: "In December, 1978, Alitalia lost
a DC9 airliner into the Mediterranean Sea and the Italian
national carrier vitally needed a replacement aircraft. Um-
berto Nordio, Alitalia's president, telephoned T. A. Wil-
son, Boeing's chairman, with a special request: could
Alitalia quickly get delivery on a Boeing 727? At the time
there was a two-year wait for such aircraft, but Boeing
juggled its production schedule and Alitalia got the plane
in a month. Mr. Nordio returned the favor six months
later, when Alitalia cancelled plans to buy McDonnell
Douglas DC10s and ordered nine 747 Jumbos [from
Boeing], valued at about $575 million."[2]

As valuable as reciprocity is, however, it ought not be
our primary motivation for providing good service. The
main reason for serving well—whether it's a waitress remembering whose steak was rare, the Maytag man fixing
the washer at 6:30 on Friday evening, or a volunteer helping in the Special Olympics—is that through service we
expand ourselves.

Once again we see the distinction between attitude and
action. Going through the motions of service is quite different from *wanting* to provide service. Many successful
companies train their staffs to serve with the attitude of
doing one's personal best—to know that service counts.
Employees of these companies realize that serving the customer is the way they serve their team, and serving their
team is the way to serve themselves.

SURRENDER CLOSE TO HOME:
FRIENDS AND FAMILY

Let's bring service to a more personal level. What does it mean to serve one's loved ones? Service—giving unstintingly to others—is basic to all successful relationships. The classic form of service is that which parents give their children, especially when the children are small. Staying awake all night putting cold compresses on a child's forehead, wiping mucus from little noses, going to see *Cinderella* instead of the latest adult drama—all of these are the surrenders that make parenthood the challenge and the delight that it is. Sometimes parents make even larger sacrifices for their children; these are the sacrifices the children never know about. The job in a distant city turned down to avoid taking the child out of school, the money not spent on a vacation for Mom and Dad so that Junior can go to camp or get his teeth fixed, the divorce delayed: all of these are surrenders for one's children.

Children also give to their parents, even though when they are young they may not realize how much joy they give their parents by loving them and by learning. When adult children support their parents with financial or emotional gifts, the parents' surrenders for their children come full circle. Brothers and sisters can serve each other in simple ways, as in helping with chores, and in deeper ways, by providing the support and friendship that only someone who has shared a lifetime of experience can give.

Moving away from the immediate circle of the family, we see that service is a prerequisite to any lasting friendship. What is friendship, after all, if not the mutual giving and receiving of confidences and support? When the father of a close friend died two days before that friend's wedding, the executive vice president of a large consulting firm left his office for two days to help arrange the funeral and to help his friend adjust to her loss. When a friend was devastated by the breakup of a long relationship shortly after she'd had a miscarriage, a couple invited her to stay with them so that she could pull herself together. Everyone hears of acts of friendship, both heroic and small. The stories are of friendship in action. In an age dominated by telephone friendship, we sometimes forget that friendship is built more on deeds than words; on giving, serving, doing for our friends as much as or more than they are doing for us. As in other cases of surrender to others, we often find that in serving our friends and loved ones the joy of expanding ourselves is greater than any cost involved in giving.

FALLING IN LOVE

> Love and harmony combine,
> And around our souls intwine,
> While thy branches mix with mine,
> And our roots together join.
> —William Blake, "Song"

"Recently I went on a one-day wilderness adventure that included this tree-climbing exercise. We were strapped securely into a harness to which a rope was attached. The rope had been looped over the top of a tree and through a pulley back down to the ground. We were asked to climb a narrow, swaying rope ladder sixty-five feet to the top of this tree, and then climb out onto a two-by-six-inch block of wood that had been optimistically labeled a platform. Then we were supposed to jump. The person on the ground holding the safety rope was responsible for pulling the rope to slow our fall. When I first saw the setup I said, 'No way.' Jumping off that tree was beyond me. I was so frightened that I cried on the guide's shoulder. At the same time, I had a sense of excitement, that if I could somehow get past my fear, I would feel wonderful on the way down. There was one man in the group whom I had connected with all day, someone who matched a lot of my images of an attractive mate. He volunteered to hold the safety rope for me. I decided to go for it in spite of my fear and began to climb the ladder.

"I'm in good physical condition, so the climb was not too difficult. Perhaps more important, as long as I was climbing, I knew I was in control. At the top, I paused to enjoy the scenery and regain my breath, and stepped out onto the platform. From there I looked down to a group of people on the ground and prepared to jump. I counted, 'One, two, three,' but I couldn't jump. The guide called up to me, 'What's going on?' and I said, 'I can't jump. I'm afraid.' 'What are you afraid of?' he asked. I looked inside myself and saw, to my surprise, an image of myself making love with a man. I didn't say anything. The guide called up again, 'Are you okay? What's going on?' and I saw myself falling into a relationship with a man, falling in love. I called down, 'This is going to sound strange, but it's about falling in love.' 'What is it about falling in love that's so frightening?' he asked. 'It's being out of control,' I replied. I looked down sixty-five feet and saw this beautiful man standing below me, holding the rope that made the difference between a graceful float to the ground and my annihilation. 'It's all right,' he said. 'I won't let you fall. Just jump.' It was one of the most intense moments of my life, standing at the top of that tree realizing how afraid I was to fall in love, and to see this man looking up at me, full of compassion, telling me it was safe to fall. I called down, 'I'm going to jump.' I counted loudly, 'One, two, three,' and tried to jump, but still my arms clung to the tree. The guide called up, 'The trust you need must come from inside you. The fear is lodged in your body, and any part of you that has not surrendered will keep you holding onto the tree. The only way to do this is to surrender 100 percent—you have to let go completely or you can't get down.' I looked down again at the man holding the rope. Finally, I knew I couldn't stay up there any longer. I looked at the peaceful landscape stretched out below me— a river wending its way through rocks, tall swaying trees, soft sunlight heading slowly toward the horizon—and I thought if I fell and died, this would be my last view on earth. Then I closed my eyes and leaned up against the tree. I took a deep breath and gathered all my energy and awareness into my body. This is it, I thought to myself. It's safe. I'm going to fall. Somehow I stepped backward off the platform. And I was flying through the air. I screamed and then felt a knot that I hadn't known was there dissolve deep in my gut. The man pulled up on the rope and stopped my fall. Very slowly he let me down, flying in the harness above the applauding group below. When I reached the ground, I felt that something new had been opened up inside me, a happy place where new adventures could grow."

This story, recounted by a young professional woman, shows how deeply the mind can identify falling in love with surrender and loss of control. For her, the focus was more on the fear than on the joy of falling; perhaps after her experience, that fear will give way to pleasure.

It's no accident that we refer to the birth of a new love as "falling." It is a fall into the excitement and the uncertainty of the unknown. Falling in love is among the most delightful surrenders, involving as it does letting go of our shell of isolation, allowing another person to become an intimate part of our lives, and flinging ourselves into the thrill of a new, life-changing relationship. There is no love without surrender. As Nathaniel Branden, author of *The Psychology of Romantic Love*, writes, "When we fall in love we experience another human being as enor-

mously important to us, enormously important to our
personal happiness. We allow that person to enter the
private world within us, which, perhaps, no one else has
ever entered or even known about. So there is a surrender,
not a surrender to the other person so much as to our feeling *for* the other person. Without that surrender love is
aborted at the outset."[3]

"When I met Drake," says Rhonda about her husband
of fourteen years, "I didn't think about protecting myself—
'I'll give up this much and see how much he gives me' and
all that. I don't know why, but I went totally open." Falling
in love is such a powerful surrender because in it we give
more of ourselves than in any other relationship. Our
physical, mental, emotional, and spiritual selves mingle
together in the creation of a new life, the life of the love
between two people. Because of this intensity, there is
more to lose—and more to gain—from falling. This par-
tially explains why falling in love can be at once so thrilling
and so frightening.

Surrender to love doesn't mean giving up who we are;
it means expanding ourselves to include another person.
We find that we can give up the desire to have a house in
our favorite neighborhood, live where our partner prefers,
and still be a whole person, or that we can let go of our
need to be right about our interpretation of a disagreement
and still feel fine. Surrendering in love helps us discover all
the things that we are not—our pet habits that drive our
partner crazy, our love of Thai food that gives our partner
gas—all that we can forgo and still be who we are. It helps
us give up ego identifications. Adapting to life with our
partner can tune us in to our essential self, which is more
than a collection of habits and opinions. The benefit,
whether we realize it at the moment or not, is that we
soften, becoming more (as the Japanese say) *shibui*,
smoothed out like a rock in a running stream.

The stronger our sense of self-esteem and the greater our self-knowledge, the easier surrender to love will be. Nathaniel Branden writes, "Sometimes I have heard a man or a woman discuss their fear of romantic love, not in terms of rejection or abandonment, but in terms of the loss of self. There is the fear that romantic love will necessitate a surrender of personal identity, a fear, in effect, that they will be taken over, body and soul, by their lover. I have never heard this fear expressed (with full seriousness) by a man or a woman with a high level of self-esteem and a strong sense of personal autonomy. On the contrary: In my experience it is precisely men and women who are self-assured and self-confident who exhibit least anxiety in surrendering to love."[4]

The initial step of falling in love is allowing it to happen at all. If we are too controlled, too analytical, too prone to calculate the potential outcome of the relationship before it's begun, we nip love in the bud and end up wondering why other people seem to be having all the fun. So the first surrender is saying, "Yes, I'll go for it, I'll fall." Many people feel that they don't have any choice about falling in love, that it's something which just "happens." Still, when we feel that irresistible tug, there is a moment when we agree not to resist the irresistible. When love affairs end, as they sometimes do, we may try to drag them out, being unwilling to confront the facts. This is when we discover how resilient we are and how able we are to let go of what is no longer ours. The Renaissance poet Michael Drayton wrote this lovely verse about letting love go when it has passed:

Since there's no help, come, let us kiss and part.
Nay, I have done; you get no more of me.
And I am glad, yea, glad with all my heart
That thus so cleanly I myself can free.

Shake hands for ever; cancel all our vows;
And when we meet at any time again,
Be it not seen in either of our brows
That we one jot of former love retain.
Now at the last gasp of Love's latest breath,
When, his pulse failing, Passion speechless lies,
When Faith is kneeling by his bed of death,
And Innocence is closing up his eyes—
    Now, if thou wouldst, when all have given him
      over,
    From death to life thou might'st him yet
      recover.

This poem also expresses the "cleanness" of dynamic surrender; that when we surrender, we do so with no strings attached. When a love affair does not pass but deepens, we face the next challenge of surrender to others in love: marriage.

MARRIAGE: THE TESTING GROUND OF SURRENDER

Let me not to the marriage of true minds
Admit impediments. Love is not love
Which alters when it alteration finds,
Or bends with the remover to remove:
O, no! it is an ever-fixèd mark
That looks on tempests and is never shaken;
It is the star to every wandering bark,
Whose worth's unknown, although his height be
    taken.
Love's not Time's fool, though rosy lips and
    cheeks
Within his bending sickle's compass come;
Love alters not with his brief hours and weeks,

But bears it out even to the edge of doom.
If this be error and upon me proved,
I never writ, nor no man ever loved.
                    —Shakespeare, Sonnet 116

"Sometimes I can see an argument coming—it's like in a chess game, you can see four or five moves ahead, or like seeing a storm coming over the horizon," says Ed, a television producer and writer. "When I'm really cool—and I hate to use that word—I can make up my mind right then to throw in my hand. It's like in poker, you just throw your cards on the table and that's the end of the game. I tell my wife, 'You're right.' And sometimes she feels like she still has to justify why she's right, so she'll explain it to me, and I just listen to her till she's finished. If I go on like this a few weeks in a row, she gets much less defensive, and my life starts getting easier. I get hugged and kissed and told I'm wonderful. Sometimes she'll even come back to me and say 'You know that time—I've been thinking about it, and you were right.' "

Marriage is the most challenging, and potentially the most rewarding, of all forms of surrender to another person. In marriage we pledge to share life with another person, to share our material, emotional, and mental resources to build a life and a family together. What greater surrender to another can there be than to link our life with another's, committing ourselves to work through the inevitable conflicts that arise? As Nathaniel Branden said to me in our conversation at his home, "In marriage, we are challenged in unique ways. I am a psychotherapist; I lead seminars in which I sometimes deal with thousands of people at one time. There is a respect in which this is child's play in comparison to what you have to do in a one-on-one relationship. It is much easier to be centered and balanced in a room with a thousand people than in your own living room. Anything irrational in my makeup, any immaturity that I could easily not be confronted with in the context of my work as a therapist or a lecturer or seminar leader will be challenged in a one-on-one relationship."

Perhaps the fear of surrendering by truly committing to another person is what stops many people in our day from entering and continuing long-term marriages. It takes a big person to surrender joyfully to the realization that at times one's spouse's welfare may come before one's own. Zen master Joshu Sasaki Roshi sums this up when he says, "There is no more difficult spiritual practice than marriage, because marriage requires both the man and the woman to give up their egos." The paradox is that if we *always* put our partner's welfare above ours, we are not surrendering—we are submitting or subjugating ourselves. Marriage is a continual process of finding the balance between surrender to the welfare of the marriage and commitment to our personal self-expression and well-being. Commitment to marriage is also commitment to a lifelong counterpoint of control and surrender.

BEYOND WIN AND LOSS

No man is an island, entire of itself; every man is a piece of the continent, a part of the main; if a clod be washed away by the sea, Europe is the less, as well as if a promontory were, as well as if a manor of thy friend's or of thine own were. Any man's death diminishes me, because I am involved in mankind; and therefore do not send to know for whom the bell tolls; it tolls for thee.

—John Donne, *Devotions Upon Emergent Occasions*

"I notice that when I give unselfishly in relationships, I seem to get back a lot, but when I feel that I'm giving in grudgingly, then nobody wins," says Allan Rudnick, investment advisor at a major investment-banking firm. Frequently we find that if we act in the other person's best interest, we end up winning, either through returned favors, through a feeling of personal growth and expansion, or because things work out fine anyway.

Dynamic surrender actually *transcends* win and loss, since it begins with neutral perception and acceptance of what is so. But surrender to others can easily become a true loss if we see it in a context of win and loss. "My ex-wife could never let a conversation end without somehow establishing that her point of view was right," says Kevin, a business consultant. "It didn't matter if we were discussing what brand of dryer to buy or what to do about a problem with one of our children. She was always trying to win. Of course, in the end she didn't win, because we split up." If all our interactions are based on win and loss or right and wrong, we can't help but lose some of the time.

But if we expand our notion of winning and losing, we may come to see surrender to others in a different light. We may see that it is hard to truly maintain a personal sense of well-being if other people are losing all around us. Multimillionaire Vidal Sassoon, speaking from his elegant office in Century City, California, says, "How can I say I'm living in dignity when I know that five miles from here there are people who aren't eating and can't work?" Other people's well-being does affect our own; it's hard for them to feel good if we're continually trying to trounce them in win-loss situations. No man is an island: When others don't feel good, we can feel good only by suppressing our awareness of their suffering, and this suppression inhibits our vitality.

The key, as I see it, is to develop that knowledge of ourselves and that grandness of spirit which will enable us to surrender when it's time to, and not to surrender when it's not time to, always maintaining a sense of how our actions affect those around us. You can tell whether your surrenders to others are wins or losses by, as always, examining your sense of well-being and the results. Do you feel good about it when you are doing it? Do you still feel good about it a few days later? Did long-term results prove that you acted in everyone's best interests?

Being put out of business, delegating authority, serving one's customers, serving the community, taking care of one's children, taking care of one's parents, and committing oneself to marriage all have this in common: They involve surrender to others, either in its life-negating or its life-serving aspect. Surrender to others, regardless of the relationship in which it takes place, means letting go of a position—in short, *giving*.

Giving our time, our energy, the substance of our lives to another can either expand or deplete us. What determines the effects that the surrender will have on us? Both the intention behind our actions and the choice of whom we surrender to. If we appear to give, serve, and surrender in the hopes of manipulating another person to reciprocate, our "surrender" may backfire, leaving us needier than before. If we give grudgingly, we are not surrendering—we are being co-opted or bartering for favors. But if we give without thought of reward, with a willingness to have the other person accept our surrender only if he feels it's in his best interest and with the desires and interests of the other person at heart, then our surrenders to others cannot but be wins, both for them and for us.

14 SEX: THE SWEET SURRENDER

To our bodies turn we then, that so
  Weak men on love reveal'd may look;
Love's mysteries in souls do grow,
  But yet the body is his book.
                    —John Donne, "The Ecstasy"

One loves the way one lives. . . . It is the great
paradox of the love world that the strongest individuals, those whose sense of themselves is most
highly developed, are most able to let go, can
most freely abandon themselves to the love world.
The very strength of their personality gives them
the assurance that they can bounce back, can reassert their individuality, and thus they do not
hesitate to surrender themselves to the duality
of the love relationship.
                    —Samuel Dunkell, *Lovelives*[1]

"Brian and I had been married for twelve years, and it
seemed that the excitement we used to feel when we made
love had gone away," says Kathleen. "It was almost mechanical. We both noticed it and started to talk about what

we could do to bring that feeling back again. Basically we were very happy together, but I think we'd just stopped paying attention to the sexual side of our relationship. Then one night after we'd spent a whole day together, just the two of us talking and taking long walks by the beach, we made love—and it was as though the whole universe exploded into an endless feeling of pleasure and love. At the height of our passion, I forgot that I was Kathleen and he was Brian. I forgot everything. There was nothing but this blaze of ecstasy sweeping through my body and his. We have felt much, much closer since then—and the passion is back."

"Sexual energy is as direct an expression of life-force as we can touch," says Robert, an entertainment attorney in Los Angeles. "We can talk about surrender to the universe and surrender to God's will, but sexual surrender is the easiest to feel." It is in our sex lives that we experience perhaps most vividly the struggle and satisfaction of both control and surrender. Sexual surrender is letting go into the pleasure and communion of the sexual encounter, an encounter blending two bodies and souls and culminating (usually) in orgasm.

In the context of making love, I see two major points regarding control and surrender. First, the more we *try* to gain control (for example, to have an erection or precipitate an orgasm), the more we lose control, finding ourselves blocked from sexual satisfaction by conscious and unconscious forces. Second, the more we simply allow our innate sexuality to surface, the more surrender—and therefore the more control—we have. We have control in the sense that we get what we want: increased sexual pleasure.

The second point is trickier than it sounds, for it does not mean "going with the flow" of sexual instincts whenever and with whomever we please. That is not surrender; it is license. As Nik Douglas and Penny Slinger, authors of

Sexual Secrets, write, "Self-indulgence is rarely the product of a natural urge. Rather, it results from a lack of emotional and psychological maturity."[2] This distinction between promiscuity and mature choice is reiterated by George Leonard, author of *The Transformation* and *The End of Sex,* when he writes, "The indiscriminate release of libido is simply the other face of sexual repression."[3] Both compulsively acting out and compulsively *not* acting out sexual desires are signs of choicelessness. Neither control nor surrender can take place unless we first develop the ability to choose.

Although most people associate sexual surrender with orgasm, one can reach profound levels of intimacy and physical satisfaction without having a physical orgasm. And even if all your limbs are flailing around and you are panting and moaning, it does not necessarily mean that you are experiencing sexual surrender. You may be or you may not be. As with other aspects of surrender, it's not the form, it's where you're coming from.

"Whenever Linda and I are having trouble in our sex life, it always develops that there was some other issue that we hadn't talked about or resolved," says Wayne. "Frequently it turns out that being sexually unresponsive is the way one of us is trying to express anger or frustration to the other. As soon as we work out the underlying issue, we're able to make love again." The emotional and physical preludes to sexual union, and of course lovemaking itself, embody the issues we face when dealing with control and surrender. In order to surrender sexually, we must trust our partner to see us at our least controlled. When making love, we surrender to our lover, to our own body, and to the spontaneous flowering of physical pleasure. Conscious sexual control, in the forms of continence and of delayed ejaculation or orgasm, builds sexual tension to the point that sexual surrender—when it finally comes—is all the sweeter.

While this is an ideal picture of sexual control and surrender, there is also a dark side. When people use sexual
intercourse to act out unresolved conflicts about domination, submission, and allowing themselves to feel pleasure,
sexuality can become a vehicle for compulsive behavior (as
with people who can experience sexual release only through
sadomasochism and bondage), repression (as with those who
are unable to reach orgasm), and manipulation and control
(as with men and women who try to force concessions from
their partners by turning the sexual faucets on and off).

THE FIRST STEP IN SEXUAL
SURRENDER

> Self-examination is vital to the evolutionary path
> of love. Only in an atmosphere of complete
> honesty can unconscious psychic impediments to
> our growth be cleared away. . . . Sexual habits
> are particularly dulling to the senses, and it is
> here that self-examination is of great value.
> —Nik Douglas and
> Penny Slinger,
> *Sexual Secrets*[4]

Satisfying sexual surrender is reached when we accept—or
surrender to—our deep psychological needs for connection,
intimacy, and full expression of our sexuality.

The prerequisite of sexual surrender, as of all surrender,
is knowing the facts. This means knowing ourself and our
own sexual nature, and knowing our partner. It means discovering and accepting innate physiological, hormonal, and
psychological characteristics and differences. It also means
taking a clear look at our partner. Who is he or she? How
does he or she feel about sexuality and love? What does he

or she want? Once we know ourselves and our partner, we
can move on to explore sexual surrender.

"I used to have a lot of rules about what was okay and
what was not okay in bed," says Cathy, an accountant. "And
I always wondered why I had a gnawing feeling of dissatis-
faction about my sex life. As my relationship with Steve
developed, I began to see that a lot of the sensations I had
decided were 'not okay' were just the sensations I was wanting. I wanted to be able to let go completely, but somehow
that was contrary to the rules I'd set for myself. Once I
realized that it was okay to want what I want, I began to
relax much more when we made love." Sexual surrender
involves coming to terms with our sexual nature as men
and women.

Many of us may be blocked from taking the first step
toward sexual surrender by a difficulty in admitting important facts about our own sexuality. For millennia it was
assumed that men are naturally aggressive and controlling
and that women are naturally passive and submissive. In
recent decades these notions have been contradicted as never
before. Men have discovered softness and receptivity within
themselves, and women have discovered assertiveness and
strength. While this is positive in that it has loosened the
hold of inflexible social roles, it also has a downside. For
just as the notion that men and women must act in certain
ways is restrictive, so is the notion that men and women
must *not* act in certain ways. In their sincere attempts not
to be "sexist," both men and women risk overlooking the
real differences between them. As George Gilder writes in
Sexual Suicide, "There are no human beings; there are just
men and women, and when they deny their divergent sexuality, they reject the deepest sources of identity and love.
They commit sexual suicide."[5]

It would be preposterous to assume that men and women

could be so radically different in physical appearance, hormonal makeup, their role in the reproductive process, and so forth, and not also be different in the way they respond to and perceive the world. Some of these differences manifest themselves sexually. Each of us experiences sexuality in a personal way, yet we cannot escape the fact that men are men and women are women. This seems obvious, but we do not always act as though it were so.

Harold, a computer systems-analyst, says, "I really think there's an underlying aggressive nature in men that enjoys attacking. Sometimes I feel like being aggressive during sex, but I block that because I'm afraid my girlfriend won't like it. Unfortunately, those aggressive impulses come out as covert hostility in other areas of the relationship." Part of the man's surrender to his own self-nature is accepting that aggressiveness is a normal component of his uniquely masculine nature. "Aggressive" need not mean violent or hostile—just more active and perhaps more dominant.

The need for aggression and control may be greater for men than for women simply because they realize, at some level, that they are indebted for their very existence to women, that they usually rely on women for support and comfort, and that they are incapable of reproducing unless they develop a relationship with a woman who will bear their child. Also, as George Gilder points out, women experience themselves as sexual beings through childbearing and nursing and are generally less dependent on sexual intercourse to reassure themselves of their sexual identity. Women are traditionally the bestowers of sexual favors; men the recipients. There is a natural inequality in favor of women when it comes to sex and love.

Moreover, centuries of biological and cultural reinforcement teach men to forge ahead, making, doing, conquering, and controlling in order to win their own self-esteem, the respect of other men, and the gifts of womanhood. Given all this conditioning, it is not surprising that men feel aggressive during sexual intercourse. This does not mean that they are unmitigatedly aggressive; in recent decades both men and women have seen that the reservoirs of love and caring within a man are no less than those within a woman. Yet a man's *expression* of love may still seem dominating or aggressive from the standpoint of traditionally feminine expressions of love.

To suggest that men accept whatever aggressive and controlling tendencies they have is in no way to suggest that they act out those impulses in the form of violence—against women or themselves. One can be sexually aggressive without being sexually violent. Those men who abuse women sexually, either through rape or violent sex, are expressing no natural aggressiveness. They are committing vicious, savage attacks against women and using sex as a weapon. But just because some men pervert their natural aggressiveness into this barbarity, it does not mean that all male aggressiveness is bad.

Just as a man need not deny his aggressive tendencies, a woman need not deny a desire to "give herself" to a man. The physical act of intercourse clearly reflects a process of control and surrender, one in which the man appears to control and the woman appears to surrender. By reveling in her role in the sexual act and in reproduction, a woman can rediscover the true power that is hers *because* of her ability to surrender. Generations of women have achieved tremendous, if not obvious, control over the values and life-styles of their families. While the freedom to earn equal pay and achieve self-expression and satisfaction through a career is a tremendous breakthrough for modern women, we need not throw out the old-fashioned joys of womanhood in the bargain. Part of those old-fashioned joys is being pursued, chosen, and adored. It's hard to pursue someone who is already pursuing. Although contemporary

women are still developing their ability to "take charge,"
being cast in the role of the one who surrenders is potentially a woman's greatest asset. Expanding ourselves as human beings means expanding our horizons of both control
and surrender—not choosing one over the other.

WHEN MORE CONTROL IS LESS

"For a long time I couldn't even allow a man to touch me,
much less make love to me," says Rene. "I was too afraid of
being emotionally hurt." Surrender to the possibility of
having a sexual encounter is the first step of sexual surrender; this is followed by surrender within the experience
itself. There is no relationship without some degree of surrender. This is especially so with sexual relationships, for
in sexual congress we cannot help but reveal ourselves more
fully than we do in daily life. If we allow ourselves to feel
anything at all, our mask of civilized politesse will drop
away, even if only at the instant of orgasm. As Wallace, a
screenwriter, says, "During sex, a more primitive part of
the nervous system takes over. But then the mind comes in
with things like 'Should I come now?' 'She probably wants
me to do this, but she might not like this,' or other thoughts
like anger or uncertainty about the woman and the relationship. But I think that true control is not having to
control at all—letting our inner nature take over without
being governed by thought." Once again we see the paradox
of control and surrender—it takes mental self-control to be
able to let go of the worried or wisecracking mind and
allow one's sexual instincts to come out. Letting go of the
controlling mind also means giving up our hunger to create
a good impression. Willingness to reveal oneself is an integral part of surrender to others, and particularly of sexual
surrender.

An unwillingness or inability to surrender may manifest itself as impotence or premature ejaculation in a man and orgasmic dysfunction in a woman. This is another case in which having too much control really means having no control. In fact, the person who is able to surrender to the experience of lovemaking and allow orgasm to happen has more control than the person who suppresses sexual excitement as it begins to stir. The fear of *not* being in control can lead men to suffer terribly when confronted by the prospect of letting themselves enjoy sex. As Masters and Johnson write in *Human Sexual Inadequacy*: "With each opportunity for sexual connection the immediate and overpowering concern is whether or not he will be able to achieve an erection. Will he be capable of 'performing' as a 'normal man'? He is constantly concerned not only with the achieving but also with maintaining an erection or quality of erection sufficient for intromission. . . . To over-simplify, it is his concern which discourages the natural occurrence of erection. . . . Many men contending with fears for sexual function have distorted this basic natural response pattern to such an extent that they literally break out in cold sweat as they approach sexual opportunity."[6]

The more you worry about it, the less it happens: What's a fellow to do? Sexual difficulties often point up an important distinction—between control that springs from fear of losing control and control that is based on awareness of oneself and one's sexuality, on the ability to choose how one will respond to one's sexual desires.

IN BED WITH YOUR EYES OPEN: CONSCIOUS SEX

While a rigid need to control may lead to ritualized sex practices (always taking one sexual position, needing props such as lingerie or sex gadgets before feeling any arousal) and orgasmic dysfunction for men and women, conscious control creates pathways to sexual bliss. In Tibetan and Chinese sexual yoga (Tantric) practices, there is tremendous emphasis on the man's ability to control his ejaculation. Ideally, the man withholds his semen and holds firm for the woman, who is supposed to enjoy as many orgasms as possible. Then, in his own sweet time, the man has his orgasm. But this idea is hardly confined to the Orient. As George Gilder writes, "The man must control his actions to enjoy intercourse most fully. To best serve his partner and not ejaculate prematurely, he must follow a gradual, managed trajectory to climax, while the woman will best enjoy herself and her partner if she loses control, if she completely relaxes, and allows climactic contractions to arise in her,"[7] Although it appears on the surface that the man represents control and the woman surrender, the goal is not to polarize the sexes into controllers and surrenderers, but to harmonize them.

According to the Tantric way of thinking, the man reaches sexual harmony through controlling his ejaculation, and the woman reaches it through having a rising tide of orgasms until she becomes a delightedly exhausted bundle of cooing satisfaction. The man knows that his control is giving his lover pleasure, and the woman knows that her avid response is pleasing her man. Experiencing sexuality in their different ways, they reach a harmony of mutual giving in which both man and woman are satisfied.

Tantric sex is based on applying optimal combinations of control and surrender: The more control the man has over his ejaculation, the more surrender is possible for the woman. And the more the woman surrenders, the more pleasure both man and woman feel. "It's my pleasure when the woman has a lot of orgasms, because I am giving her pleasure," says a prominent European film star. As the

seventh-century Chinese physician Li Tung Hsuan wrote,
"A man should cultivate the ability to delay his ejaculation
until his love partner is fully satisfied."[8]

Some Oriental texts go so far as to suggest that men
make love many times over a period of weeks without
ejaculating. Those who have practiced this say that once
they have mastered ejaculatory control, their sex life gives
them all the pleasure of ejaculatory sex without the physical
depletion that follows repeated emission of semen. One
master of Chinese sexual yoga writes, "I can say that sex
without ejaculation is also a release of tension but without
the explosion. It is a pleasure of peace not of violence, a
sensuous and lastingly satisfying melting into something
larger and more transcendent than oneself. It is a feeling of
wholeness, not of separation; a merging and a sharing, not
an exclusive, private and lonely spasm."[9] The idea that
every sexual experience *must* culminate in orgasm is one
more way we try to program pleasure into our lives—and
thereby risk programming it out.

Sexual fidelity is another aspect of sexual control. For
several decades the view prevailed that having multiple
sexual partners meant having greater sexual freedom, but
people who have experimented (both men and women)
usually say that a string of casual lovers makes them feel
cheated and empty in the end. *Cosmopolitan* magazine reported in 1980 after a survey of more than 106,000 women,
"So many readers wrote negatively about the sexual revolu-
tion, expressing longings for vanished intimacy and the now
elusive joys of romance and commitment that we began to
sense that there might be a sexual counter-revolution under-
way in America."[10] Restricting oneself to one cherished
partner may help create the trust so essential to an intimate
sexual relationship. Some people claim that a long-term
relationship creates sexual boredom, but it can just as easily
create a safe space for sexual freedom and relaxation.

"There's something comforting about being married," says Martha, a woman who had many sexual relationships before she married in her early forties, "because we know that even if the sex isn't wonderful one day, we can try again tomorrow. When I was single, I never had that security, so I was constantly worrying, 'How is it? Am I doing okay?' With Ted I feel safe to do anything—including not worry and not come."

The conscious control we exercise in choosing and remaining faithful to our partner and the control the man develops over his physical reactions pay off in the form of greater freedom for sexual surrender.

TRY, TRY, TRY: THE BANE OF
SEXUAL SURRENDER

> If spontaneity is difficult for a person to achieve in other areas of existence, so in the sexual act that person's approach is likely to be carefully contained, clinging to a set routine that makes surprise unlikely. If an individual is upset by physicality itself, by body contact, by interpenetration, then sexual relations will probably be considerably constricted. A fear of commitment will be shown not only in the person's overall way of treating the love partner but also in the very alignment of the body during sex. And if a person is afraid of pleasure, of sensory gratification, another characteristic set of defenses will be erected.
>
> —Samuel Dunkell, Lovelives[11]

The idea that orgasm can be forced is typical of the thinking of a frigid woman. We have seen that, because she is basically frightened, basically mistrusts her husband's love of her and her own femininity, she has to feel that she is "in control" all the time. The trouble with that standpoint is that in real orgasm a woman must be out of control; must willfully, delightedly desire to be entirely so.

—Marie N. Robinson,
*The Power of Sexual
Surrender*[12]

"Susan and I tried everything to make our sex life better," says Michael, a producer of corporate publicity films. "We went to weekend workshops, encounter groups, and sex therapists, read pornography together in bed, and rented X-rated video cassettes. But it seemed like the more we tried, the more stilted our sex life became. There was always a period at the beginning when we really would open up more, communicate our desires and fears, and all that, but within a few weeks we got hung up on the idea of 'doing it right'—the way the workshop leader or the therapist or the book said. And then it was downhill all the way."

The quickest way to block sexual satisfaction and surrender is to try to do sex "right." Many people make love with internal voices telling them what to do and when to do it, always asking whether what they're doing is "working." On top of this are the voices of numerous others—their mother, their father, their ex-wife or ex-husband, their teachers, their therapist, and all the friends who supposedly have nothing but superlative sex. Who could relax with all this racket going on?

Barriers to sexual surrender begin and end in our mind. It takes mental self-control to turn to the whole inner peanut gallery and get it to shut up. Before we can induce all those voices to be quiet, we have to surrender to them at least once —to listen unabashedly to what they are saying. If we try to press ahead and ignore them, they'll get louder and louder until any physical spontaneity is stymied. Those who think they have no hang-ups about sex—it's just that they keep getting stuck with lousy partners—may be shocked to discover how many caustic kibitzers reside in their own minds. Having listened to these voices, we are in a position to thank them very much for their input and then tell them to be quiet. Control (to make ourselves stop running from the voices in our heads) leads to surrender (seeing what's already there), which leads to control (not allowing the contents of our mind to dominate our behavior), which leads to surrender (allowing enjoyable sex). Sounds great: Who's going first?

ORGASMIC SURRENDER: EVERYBODY'S DREAM

According to Marie N. Robinson, "The ability to achieve normal orgasm can be called the physical counterpart of psychological surrender. In most cases of true frigidity it follows on a woman's surrender of her rebellious and infantile attitudes as the day the night. It is the sign that she has given up the last vestige of resistance to her nature and has embraced womanhood with soul *and* body."[13] Orgasm is the ultimate moment of sexual surrender. It brings release, a sense of unbounded flowing into and through one's lover, and a flood of serenity and well-being that lasts long after the final throbs of sexual pleasure fade away. It is the closest thing to mystical surrender that many of us reach. During orgasm, it is impossible to maintain a pretense of control; in fact, orgasm is the very antithesis of control. Like other forms of surrender, orgasm is something we build up to, something that begins with the decision to make love and then grows stronger as we allow our innate sexuality and capacity for pleasure to take over. Nearly everyone can have an orgasm unless layers of cerebral control block its free flow. In short, orgasm happens when we get out of its way.

Giving up resistance, experiencing unity, allowing tensions to dissipate in paroxysms of pleasure—no wonder everybody wants great sex. Dozens of books have been written about it, talk-show psychologists lecture rapt audiences about it, people pay therapists to learn how to have an orgasm or to improve the ones they have. Some people search for the perfect orgasm the way others search for the perfect sushi. Why does it seem so elusive? Why has it become such "an issue"?

Perhaps the fixation on orgasms and all things sexual exists because lovemaking is one of the last areas in which we allow ourselves to experience pleasure; it is a culturally sanctioned way to act out our unprogrammed natural instincts. We're trained *not* to act on most of our spontaneous physical impulses: we're not supposed to be violent; we're not supposed to lie in bed all day if we feel like it; if we have to go to the bathroom in the middle of a meeting, we are supposed to "hold it." But sex is different. We want sex to be the area of our greatest surrender—but ironically we try to experience this ultimate surrender by planning and worrying about it the way we do about everything else. "People try to do all these things to get orgasms, but that's how they get out of touch," says Matthew, an advertising copywriter in New York.

Unfortunately, the more we *try* to surrender into orgasm, the more problems we are likely to have with it. To quote Marie N. Robinson again: "There can, it is clear, be no crossed fingers about such yielding, no reservations in such surrender. As one thinks of it one can certainly feel why, of all the steps in the process of yielding, of surrendering, the orgasm should be last. To those who are moving toward it the experience often remains for a time elusive because its very totality, its uncompromising demand that the whole being be swept up in the experience, remains somewhat frightening."[14]

Any fears of surrender we are holding on to, particularly fears of sexual surrender and release, will show up just when we want them least: when we attempt to reach orgasm. If we are separating ourselves from the experience, stepping aside to judge, evaluate, and plan our next move, it is impossible to surrender and enjoy it. One sexual interlude may include orgasm; another may not. One may be languorous and sensual; another may be fast and hard. What's the difference if both adults consent and enjoy it? Sexual surrender comes when we let go of our preconceptions about how it "ought" to be.

SWEET SEXUAL SURRENDER

Sexual surrender involves knowing ourselves, knowing our partners, and accepting our own sexual needs and nature. Trying to "achieve" sexual surrender probably does more to subvert it than forgetting about it altogether, but a certain amount of self-control can enhance it. Sexual surrender is no different from other types of surrender, except that it may be more euphoric. It requires us to accept facts, to let go of our attachment to form (you don't *have* to have an orgasm every time!), and to trust that a healthy process once begun will reach its own climax and conclusion. Reaching a state of sexual surrender means wresting ourselves from the notion that we *are* our sex life or our sexuality: We are more than that. Once we've realized this, the presence or absence of a particular stroke seems far less important.

Sexual surrender happens when we have recovered our ability to choose what we will do and how we will do it. If we must have sex at a particular interval or in a particular way, we don't have enough control over ourselves to begin to surrender. Fixations about sex lead to compulsion; compulsion means having no choice. This frequently devolves into having no sex, either.

Western culture has been through several decades of "loosening up" about sex. Perhaps now it's time to loosen up about loosening up: Maybe nonstop sex is not all that important. In a recent psychology experiment, researchers implanted electrodes into the pleasure centers of the brains of a group of rats. Every time an electrical charge was sent through the wire, the rat jumped and experienced intense pleasure. The experiment was set up so that the rat had to press a certain lever in order to receive the charge. The experimenters found that as long as they sent the charge through the electrode, the rats would keep pressing the lever until they were too exhausted to move. Some of the rats killed themselves with fatigue this way. Advertisers and those in the media know that that if they mention sex the public will jump, just like the rats pressing the lever. If we jump every time someone mentions or alludes to sex, are we in control? Is this choice? How can we hope to experience sexual surrender if we are locked into compulsive reactions to sexual innuendo?

Like other surrenders, sexual surrender involves nonattachment to results. Choose your partner wisely and then live in the moment, whether or not the experience fits your mental picture of how it ought to look. What began as torrid lovemaking may end as hours of intimate conversation. All forms are fluid: If you depend on them to be unchanging, you will be disappointed. Surrender to the moment and let it take its own form.

In sexual relations, great control leads to great surrender. By prolonging the sexual act and learning to delay the orgasm, the ultimate pleasure of the act is increased many times over. Once again we see the pattern that the more

fully one is able to control, the more fully one can surrender, and that control when carried to its peak ultimately
dissolves into a blissful surrender. By dynamically balancing
the forces of control and surrender, we can also experience
within ourselves what we experience through sexual union
with another: the creation of new life.

15 BRINGING IT ALL TOGETHER: SURRENDER TO LIFE

Human life is nothing but the expression of
God's exuberance.
—Anthony de Mello

The further one travels, the less one knows.
—Lao Tzu

WINNERS KNOW HOW TO LET GO

In the course of writing this book I interviewed leaders in
some of this country's major industries. *Every one* of these
leaders expressed similar sentiments about the nature of
control and the value of dynamic surrender. They know
that clear perception of the facts is the only place to start
and that letting go is often the best place to finish. They
may have advocated surrender within a context of either
corporate or personal control, but each one understood the
necessity of delegation, the primacy of service, the power of
letting their subordinates rise, and the value of letting go
positions that are no longer tenable. They also know that
they cannot afford to be personally attached to the outcome
of every situation. As Bob Steiner, director of public rela-

tions for California Sports, which owns the Los Angeles Lakers, Kings, and Lazers, says, "Great players are not afraid to lose." When winners let go, they do so cleanly, without regret. They know how to give under pressure without breaking.

Publisher Malcolm Forbes is an accomplished balloonist, a motorcycle enthusiast, and a collector of fine art. He says, "My feeling is that while you're alive you ought to embrace life, to live it. And to do that you have to follow your bent. I think that to keep control, you let it go. They're not contradictory really—you almost require one to get the other." We need both control and surrender, but we need them in dynamic balance.

KEY ELEMENTS OF SURRENDER

You already know how to surrender: You pull to the right when an ambulance screams down the street, adapt your product to the desires of your market, allow your children and loved ones to learn by making mistakes. You were born in surrender—nobody asked you to sign up for your preferred time and place of birth, but you arrived when the time came. You will die in surrender, too, with about as little control over death as you had over birth. If you want to surrender more, all you need do is consciously expand your ability to surrender in other areas of life.

The first step of surrender is to *see what's so*, understanding and accepting things as they really are. Once we have identified the factors we can control and those we cannot, we can make allowances for, or try to get around, the uncontrollable and go to work on what we *can* control. Seeing what's so means letting go of all our wishes, hopes, fantasies, fears, and expectations about a situation. Thus, it is preceded by surrender of the ego, the part of us that's always figuring out how things *ought* to be. No problem, right? We'll just throw that ego out and sail into dynamic surrender. Theoretically, it *is* no problem, but practically, which is where most of us live, it often is.

All of us have blind spots of desire that prevent us from seeing or accepting things as they are. "Sometimes I have such a strong feeling that a particular customer is going to buy that I overlook all the evidence to the contrary," says Wayne, a sales representative for a major copying-machine corporation. "I can remember calling a prospect six or seven times before finally saying to myself, 'They *really* aren't interested.' " We overlook facts in our personal relationships as well. "I have a friend who would wait weeks for a man she'd met at a party to call her, thinking that he must have liked her so much, he was afraid to call," says Diane. "She just couldn't accept that he didn't want to see her." In certain areas, all of us overlook the obvious.

You may not always be able to see what's so. But you can at least *commit yourself* to seeing it. Out of that commitment to knowing the truth comes the courage to set aside the opinions and needs of the ego and to accept reality.

Another key to surrender is *self-knowledge*. No one can surrender in a life-serving way unless he knows who he is. You cannot give away what you do not first have, and you cannot surrender yourself unless first you have yourself to give.

Then there is *nonattachment to results*. How can we claim to have surrendered in any absolute sense until we reach a point of dispassion about the results of our actions? Any lingering attachments to having things our way hook us back into barter and control.

When you *do* decide to surrender, do it gracefully, with *fluidity*. A sense of free flow marks the wholehearted "yes" that true surrender is.

And when you surrender, *choose life-serving over life-*

negating surrenders. This means that the object of your surrender (if the surrender has an object) contributes to your sense of expansion and well-being. Surrender to loving a person who is equally willing to surrender to his or her love for you would be a life-serving surrender. Surrender to a new job that will cause you to expand your leadership abilities is also a life-serving surrender. Surrender to a lover or leader who tries to manipulate you and rob you of your personal power or who insists that you do all the surrendering and he do all the controlling, is a life-negating surrender.

If your surrender is internally focused, you can surrender to some larger aspect of yourself. Suppose that you have a lot of work to do—a report, your taxes, anything—and you don't want to do it. No one will know immediately if you don't do it, but you promised yourself you would complete it today. You can let go of the part that says "I don't want to" in favor of the part that says "I promised myself I would finish this." Or suppose you have a friend whose husband has just walked out on her. She calls you several times a day for two weeks, expressing her anguish and anger about the breakup. You of course have other things to do. Besides, listening to her reminds you of *your* last heartbreak, which you really don't want to be reminded of. One part of you wants to tell her to leave you alone. Another part has compassion and knows that when you were in her position, you had to rely on friends for support because your primary source of support had just walked out of your life. You can let go of the part that wants to close up in favor of the part that is compassionate. (If you feel that you can't help her anymore, you can support her in getting professional counseling.) Your surrender is to being a good friend. The extent to which we benefit from our surrender depends on how fully we surrender and on the degree to which our surrender is life expanding.

If you want to encourage yourself to surrender more, just consider the cost of not surrendering. In business, no surrender means no delegation, no new ideas, no risk taking. In relationships, no surrender means alienation, no sharing, none of the excitement of love. Over time, this cost is hardly worth the meager pride that comes from claiming "I have not surrendered."

PRACTICE MAKES SURRENDER

Think of the courage it takes for any of us to make it through life—the broken loves, the unmaterialized career plans, the thousands of expectations and goals that over the years go unfulfilled. Would it be easier to go through all this if we were more fluid? Of course. That is one of the many reasons to *practice* surrender.

Although there is no "how to" in surrender, practice is one thing you *can* do. There is a saying: Nobody ever got worse at anything by practicing. Take surrender breaks. Disengage from the world twenty or thirty minutes a day through meditation, brisk exercise, puttering in the garden, staring at the sea, or whatever. If you don't have time for a long break, then simply breathe deeply a few times. That alone will enable you to step outside the cares of the moment.

Practice letting go. Find the boundaries of your fear of surrender: the levels of intimacy to which you never travel, the things you never allow yourself to have. Find them, and then take one step beyond them. A friend moves to another city, you feel betrayed and want to close up a little more to the next new friend—take note of that boundary, feel around its edges, and then stretch, stretch, stretch. You are offered something fabulous and new in work, travel, or another area of life, and you hold back: Observe the boundary of what you're willing to have and act as though it weren't there. Jump.

Essentially, the only thing to surrender is our "ego," the aspect of ourselves that keeps us locked into an identification with our opinions, feelings, and judgments. Letting go of this powerful mechanism within us may feel like death, but it isn't. Even after we've let go of our attachment to the ego, it continues to offer its interpretations of and comments on everything we say and do. That little voice in our heads will never shut up for long. But after we've let go, we don't pay attention to it anymore. Surrendering the ego is no more like the death of our true selves than pruning a branch is the death of the whole tree. So why not try it? As Meister Eckhart said, we must let go of who we think we are in order to be the person we can become.

KEY ELEMENTS OF CONTROL

But right at the bottom of the problem of control is "How am I to get out of my own way?" If I showed you a system—"Let's all practice getting out of our own way"—it would only turn into another form of self-improvement. . . . In the phraseology of Zen Buddhism, "You cannot achieve this by thinking, you cannot achieve this by not thinking." Getting out of your own way comes about only when doing so ceases to be a matter of choice, because you see that there is nothing else for you to do. In other words, it happens when you see that doing something about your situation is not going to help, and that trying *not* to do anything about it is equally not going to help you. Then where do you stand?

> You are nonplussed. You are simply reduced to
> watching and letting it be.
> —Alan Watts,
> *The Way of Liberation*[1]

If we are unable to choose whether or not to control, we are
not in control. That's why we say that *control implies
choice*. We cannot choose unless we choose from more than
one option. If we think that control is our only option, we
don't have choice. Many people do not realize that *not
being in control is an acceptable choice*: What most experience when they realize they no longer have to be in control all the time is an overwhelming sense of relief.

Paradoxically, the more we try (through struggle and
effort) to gain control, the more we lose it. And the more
we let go (of attachment to outcome and need to dominate),
the more we get it.

Unlike surrender, *control manifests itself through form
and discipline*: patterns of speech, patterns of movement,
patterns of thought. "Uncontrolled" is nearly synonymous
with "formless" or "undisciplined." Definite form evidences
control.

Shrewd, effective control takes into account the realities
of a situation and works with them rather than against
them. *Control begins with acceptance of facts.* No one ever
made a dream come true by being dreamy about the facts he
was starting with. He may have viewed the facts differently
than others, or seen possibilities within them that others
overlooked, or seen that what others thought were facts
were nothing but commonly held assumptions (as with political or religious revolutionaries who ignored the "fact"
that no one could topple the establishment, and then went
ahead and did it), but no one makes it in life without beginning from a reality base.

THE DYNAMISM OF CONTROL
AND SURRENDER

As marvelous and essential as control is, the fact is that we cannot control everything. If control is our only weapon against chaos and defeat, we simply cannot control enough. But here the relationship between control and surrender comes into play. As Nancy Zapolski says, "True control is doing nothing, adding nothing, letting things be. So much energy is released from the nonresistance that a vacuum is created, which creates the momentum for action." The locomotive force of an automobile engine is produced by the interaction of the upstrokes and the downstrokes of the pistons; too much of one or another stroke leads to a clankety car. In a similar way, our power is enhanced by alternating between control and surrender. Too much control or too much surrender sets us off balance.

Frances Vaughan, author of *Awakening Intuition*, said in a discussion with me, "The question of surrender and control takes on another meaning in the context of psychotherapy. It's a question of balance. If someone comes into therapy and is suffering from a lot of suppression and is overly controlled in some way, then we encourage him or her to let go, to surrender in a certain sense. But on the other hand if a person comes in and is feeling perpetually victimized because he or she is unable to be assertive, then he or she is encouraged to take control of his or her life and to move assertively. I don't think there's an absolute answer one way or the other, but we need to look at the dynamic balance between our own particular way of handling surrender and control." We may swing from the pole of control to the pole of surrender, but to be as effective as we can be, it's essential to maintain equilibrium.

As Jewish scholar Jonathan Omer-Man said to me, "One

cannot live in a state of surrender. We must always be on guard against our own self-destructiveness and self-deception. This is what discipline gives us—the ability to recognize self-deception, to recognize self-destructiveness, to know where we are. You can only know where you are when you have some coordinates. If you are in the middle of the ocean and you are just floating, you have no idea where you are." By applying control, we create a structure within which to define ourselves—and to act.

MEETING OUR ULTIMATE GOALS

Hank, an American who fought in Vietnam, says that American and South Vietnamese soldiers were periodically ordered to locate presumed Vietcong agents among the South Vietnamese population and to kill them. If an agent's wife and family were present, they were to be killed too. According to Hank, "Once we were assigned to kill someone who our Vietnamese sources had reported was giving information to the Vietcong. We took a riverboat until we found his tiny village. As we sailed past, we saw a group of Vietnamese sitting on the bank. One of them matched the snapshot of the man we were supposed to kill. He was a little seventy-eight-year-old man with bags under his eyes. We stopped the boat, landed, and took off after him. As soon as he knew we'd recognized him, he ran. We followed him to his house.

"Three men stood outside the house to back me up, and I pushed through the door: I was supposed to kill them. I took aim. The old man stopped and looked around his home—at his wife and children and grandchildren crouching terrified by the flickering light of the kerosene lamp, knowing that they were all about to die. Then he walked up to me and stuck his finger in the barrel of my Uzi submachine gun. He just looked at me. A few seconds went by. I shook him off. I shot ten or fifteen rounds into the roof and gestured the whole family to lie down. I left. That was my last raid. I applied to go back to the States."

Through his courageous willingness to surrender his life, the old man gained control over the situation that threatened him. Frequently we find that the best way to gain control and meet our ultimate goal is to surrender.

In Search of Excellence: Lessons From America's Best Run Companies is a study of the factors most consistently present among the most profitable and long-lived companies in America. In the closing chapter, the authors, Thomas J. Peters and Robert J. Waterman, Jr., point to "simultaneous loose-tight properties" as the summary of all they found most conducive to success:

> Organizations that live by the loose-tight principle are on the one hand rigidly controlled, yet at the same time allow (indeed, insist on) autonomy, entrepreneurship, and innovation from rank and file. . . . But at the same time, a remarkably tight—culturally driven/controlled—set of properties marks the excellent companies. . . .
>
> The "rules" in the excellent companies have a positive cast. They deal with quality, service, innovation, and experimentation. Their focus is on building, expanding, the opposite of restraining; whereas most companies concentrate on controlling, limiting, constraint. We don't seem to understand that rules can reinforce positive traits as well as discourage negative ones, and that the former kind are far more effective.[2]

This loose-tight quality is similar to a surrendered-controlled state of being—one in which both letting go and holding on have their place.

Control can provide the structure for surrender just as the skeleton provides the structure for the body. Without structure, what we call surrender may turn out to be jelly-boned spinelessness. So in a sense, form does matter. Control and discipline are form. A person cannot be a great swimmer, or skier, or pianist, or singer, or writer, or actor, or stockbroker, or accountant without first mastering the appropriate form. Only after the strokes, the scales, the grammar, the technique, and the laws have been mastered is one free to ply one's art. Imagine anyone you know who is outstanding at his work who has not mastered the form of it. Imagine Artur Rubinstein playing the piano without first mastering every aspect of piano technique; imagine Martina Navratilova playing tennis with an awkward stroke. Beethoven spent twenty-five years mastering counterpoint and harmony; Picasso spent years mastering draftsmanship before he transformed the rules of painting. Excellence does not happen without the discipline of form. Just as a river gathers strength from being held within its banks, so each of us gathers strength from the forms of control we master.

In the greatest companies and the strongest relationships, control through surrender is the key to power. Control by its very nature is static; surrender by its very nature is fluid. While there is no denying the importance and value of control, the purpose of control is more to create a vehicle for surrender than to exist as an end in itself. A tight system of controls makes full-blooded surrender possible—but never forget that it is not the control that causes creativity and expansion. It is the surrender, that free-flowing movement within the structure of control, that causes growth. "Doesn't professional writing require a tremendous ability to let go?" asked Roz of her friend Elaine, who was just having her sixth book published. "It takes a lot of letting go, but also a lot of discipline. The more disciplined I get, the more freedom I have to write." Control is a means, not an end in itself; it is a means to facilitate surrender.

The more perfectly we master form, the more freely we can create within it. However, if *all* we master is form, we are left with a dead structure. The whole purpose of form is to create strong boundaries within which spirit can flow; the whole purpose of control is to create a strong crucible for surrender. The discipline of musical scales and harmonies creates the context for musical genius; the controls of perspective and paint set the challenge for great painting; the constraints of law and the marketplace form the structure in which new products are produced and sold; and the set of agreements within a relationship establish the environment in which love can flower. Perfect control enables us to reach perfect surrender.

Jewish mystical literature uses the image of light and vessels (in Hebrew, *Or ve-Kaylim*) to express the relationship between form and spirit. The "vessel" represents form; in practice, it can be a set of behavioral norms, regulations set by civil law, the rules of a particular business, or the agreements that define a personal relationship. Anything with a structure or discipline is a vessel. The "light" is life-force, spirit, creativity, vitality. Although in itself it is formless, it is the driving force that gives life to form. Jonathan Omer-Man explains it this way: "According to this idea, every aspect of creation is made up of these two components. The totality of the universe and every part of it, the Torah, our social and religious institutions, and each individual human being are conceived as being light and vessels. Light is the divine essence, and the vessels are the form, or the form and matter, into which it is poured. Light is the soul and the vessel is the body. Now, the divine light cannot be seen or manifest without a vessel; without form, the divine light is lost, for it either dissipates or, even worse, attaches itself to inappropriate vessels. The opposite is true as well; vessels without light become heavy, meaningless dross. According to this model, our task is to achieve a proper balance, in our lives and in the world, between light and vessels."

Our ability to control, and the forms through which we manifest our control, can be seen as the vessels. The fluid, dynamic spirit of surrender is the light. Without a strong vessel (created through self-discipline), the conscious choice to adhere to ethical norms, and a commitment to mastering the rules and forms of whatever our business is in life, we risk dissipating the light of surrender. The stronger we make our vessel, the freer we will be to surrender within it. The two must develop in tandem: As we strengthen the form, we allow a greater and greater flow of surrender. If either aspect develops out of balance with the other, we ourselves are out of balance.

Form without spirit is dead, and spirit without discipline is dissipated. We need both: form and spirit, discipline and creativity, control and surrender. Without control and discipline there would be no structure to hold our surrender. Yet without the flow of surrender, what is the structure for?

The quest for control seems so important at times that we lose sight of control's purpose. Control is not an end in itself; it is a means, a way of stabilizing ourselves so that surrender can take place. So if you want to control, go ahead. But ask yourself, "What surrender is this preparing me for?"

Let us commit ourselves to surrender—relinquish completely, without a backward glance or a hook of attachment —life-negating patterns. Let us commit ourselves to look for, probe, and find the source of life within ourselves that enables us to give ourselves utterly to life, to embrace things as they are and work with them, patiently building, like the nautilus with his shell, larger and larger forms into which we can pour the light of our surrender. Then, after patient practice, we may reach the point where we can throw off the shell and bare ourselves to that blazing light which transcends both control and surrender. The first step toward that is surrender to life.

Notes

CHAPTER 1   *Always the Question: To Hold On or Let Go?*

1. Quoted in Reshad Feild, *The Last Barrier* (New York: Harper and Row, 1976), 76.

CHAPTER 3   *Holding the Line: Self-Control*

1. Hans Selye, *Stress without Distress* (New York: Signet/New American Library, 1974), 14.

CHAPTER 6   *"Why Did I Do That?": Unconscious Control*

1. Carl Jung, "The Phenomenology of the Self," in *The Portable Jung*, ed. Joseph Campbell (New York: Viking, 1971), 147.

2. Nathaniel Branden, *The Psychology of Romantic Love* (Los Angeles: J. P. Tarcher, 1980), 134.

3. Quoted in Stephen Levine, *Who Dies? An Investigation into Conscious Living and Conscious Dying* (New York: Anchor/Doubleday, 1980), 15.

CHAPTER 7   *Controlling Your Life: A Matter of Practice*

1. Sören Kierkegaard, *Fear and Trembling/Repetition*, vol. 6 of *Kierkegaard's Writings*, ed. and trans. Howard V. Hong

and Edna H. Hong (Princeton: Princeton University Press, 1983), 47.

CHAPTER 8   *Controlling Others: The Impossible Dream*

1. Alan Watts, *The Way of Liberation: Essays and Lectures on the Transformation of the Self*, ed. Mark Watts and Rebecca Shropshire (New York: Weatherhill, 1983), 62.

2. Elizabeth Forsythe Hailey, *A Woman of Independent Means* (New York: Viking Press/Avon, 1978), 259.

CHAPTER 9   *Surrender: What's Good about It?*

1. Carl Sandburg, *The People, Yes* (New York: Harcourt, Brace & World, 1936), 18.

2. Watts, *Liberation*, 56.

3. Jean-Pierre de Caussade, *Abandonment to Divine Providence*, trans. John Beevers (New York: Doubleday Image Books, 1975), 21.

4. Quoted in Perry N. Whitall, *A Treasury of Traditional Wisdom* (New York: Simon and Schuster, 1969), 331.

5. Quoted in Whitall, *Treasury*, 977.

CHAPTER 10   *"I Can't Let Go!": Fear of Surrender*

1. Levine, *Who Dies?*, 4.

2. Elisabeth Kübler-Ross, *On Death and Dying* (New York: Macmillan, 1969), 114.

3. Willis Barnstone, trans., *The Poems of St. John of the Cross* (New York: New Directions, 1972), 62–65.

CHAPTER 11   *Easy Does It: Surrender Step by Step*

1. Quoted in Feild, *Barrier*, 39.

2. Levine, *Who Dies?*, 66.

3. Levine, *Who Dies?*, 35.

4. Feild, *Barrier*, 30.

CHAPTER 12   *"So How Do I Do It?": Surrender in Action*

1. Caussade, *Abandonment*, 113.

2. Leo Tolstoy, *War and Peace*, trans. Ann Dunnigan (New York: New American Library, 1968), 896.

3. Feild, *Barrier*, 60.

4. Aldous Huxley, *The Perennial Philosophy* (New York: Harper Colophon Books, 1944), 43.

5. Donovan Leitch, "Pebble and the Man," Donovan (Music) Ltd.

6. Caussade, *Abandonment*, 59.

7. Feild, *Barrier*, 53.

8. Kierkegaard, *Fear and Trembling*, 16.

9. Watts, *Liberation*, 56.

CHAPTER 13   *Surrender to Others: Win or Loss?*

1. Thomas J. Peters and Robert H. Waterman, Jr., *In Search of Excellence: Lessons from America's Best-Run Companies* (New York: Harper and Row, 1982), 16.

2. Peters and Waterman, *Excellence*, 169.

3. Branden, *Romantic Love*, 165.

4. Branden, *Romantic Love*, 167.

CHAPTER 14   *Sex: The Sweet Surrender*

1. Samuel Dunkell, *Lovelives—How We Make Love* (New York: William Morrow, 1978), 32.

2. Nik Douglas and Penny Slinger, *Sexual Secrets* (New York: Destiny Books, 1979), 63.

3. George Leonard, "The End of Sex," *Esquire*, December 1982, 74.

4. Douglas and Slinger, *Sexual Secrets*, 28.

5. George Gilder, *Sexual Suicide* (New York: Quadrangle/New York Times Books, 1973), 43.

6. William H. Masters and Virginia E. Johnson, *Human Sexual Inadequacy* (Boston: Little, Brown and Co., 1970), 11–12.

7. Gilder, *Sexual Suicide*, 38.

8. Jolan Chang, *The Tao of Love and Sex—The Ancient Chinese Way to Ecstasy* (New York: E. P. Dutton, 1979), 21.

9. Chang, *Tao of Love*, 25.

10. Quoted in Leonard, "The End of Sex," 74.

11. Dunkell, *Lovelives*, 13.

12. Marie N. Robinson, *The Power of Sexual Surrender* (New York: Signet/New American Library, 1959), 158.

13. Robinson, *Sexual Surrender*, 157.

14. Robinson, *Sexual Surrender*, 158.

CHAPTER 15   *Bringing It All Together: Surrender to Life*

1. Watts, *Liberation*, 71.

2. Peters and Waterman, *Excellence*, 318–20.

Acknowledgments

Many people contributed to this book through their love, insight, and positive criticism. It's difficult to name them all, but I'll try.

First I'd like to thank the business people, psychologists, and scholars who agreed to be interviewed and to share their thoughts on control and surrender with me: Jay D. Atlas, Ph.D., of Pomona College; George Ball; Morton O. Beckner, Ph.D., of Pomona College; Barbara Boyle of Orion Pictures; Nathaniel Branden, Ph.D.; Harry Brickman, M.D., Ph.D.; Jerry Buss, Ph.D.; Michael Crichton; Arthur Deikman, M.D.; Judith d'Ifray, of T. J. D'Ifray, Inc.; Stephen Erickson, Ph.D., of Pomona College; Herbert Fingarette, Ph.D., of the University of California at Santa Barbara; Malcolm Forbes of Forbes, Inc.; Michael Fuchs of Home Box Office International; Tetsugen Glassman Sensei; Harvey Harrison; Karen Harvey of Now, An Educational Corporation; Jas Want Khalsa, M.D.; Kim Kruglick, Esq.; Rabbi Daniel Lapin; Susan Lapin; Darryll Leiman; Kay McMurray, director of the Federal Mediation and Conciliation Service; Michael Medved; Judith Mishell, Ph.D.; Jay Olins, president of California Student Loan Finance Corporation; Jonathan Omer-Man; Judith Orloff, M.D.; Pete Peterson of Peterson, Jacobs and Co.; Alan Platt, Ph.D., of The Rand Corporation; Ernest Rossi, Ph.D.; Thomas Safran of Thomas Safran and Associates; Vidal Sassoon of Vidal Sassoon Enterprises; Hank Shapiro of Customized Information Systems; June and Jim Singer; and Nancy Zapolski of Werner Erhard and Associates.

I also thank the many friends who shared their thoughts, life experiences, and feelings about control and surrender: Malinda Benedek; Irene Borger; David Brenner; Joy Brenner; Abby, Margo, and Jake Brenner; Grace Brenner; Rebecca Brenner; Christen Brown; Rona Cherry; G. Tom Collins; Ernest Del; Robert Dellenger; Tom Drucker; J. J. Ebaugh; Matt Geller; Wayne Gray; Rick Green; Philip Goldberg; Dorien Grunbaum; Allen Hershberg; Carole Isenberg; Jim Kearney; Savely Kramarov; Marie-Denise Kratsios; Paula Levenbach; Bill and Sandy Leyton; Marsha Mayer; Priscilla Mayer; Harry Medved; Orson Mozes; Sally Olins; Suzy Prudden; Alan Rudnick; Jeanette Sassoon; Marcia Seligson-Drucker; Frank Shaw; Patricia Shaw; DeWayne Snodgrass; Roy Strassman; Deborah Swartz; and Alexandra Tuttle.

The final editing of the manuscript was done by John Radziewicz of Harcourt Brace Jovanovich with the assistance of Naomi Grady. I am deeply grateful to both of them for their insights and support.

I especially thank my agent and friend, Martha Sternberg, who has supported this project in every way possible from inception to completion. Special thanks also to Howard Sandum, who initially saw the value of this project for publication, and to Jonathan Omer-Man, who understood this book long before I began to write it.

To all who contributed their experiences, thoughts, and energy, I am deeply grateful. I accept full responsibility for any errors or omissions in the text.

Venice, California
May 1984